James Reaney's ten emblems are among the most mysterious of his works. Are they poems? works of art? performances? And how did they emerge from Reaney's fabled 'playbox,' the imaginative source of everything he did? In this rich new study, *The Emblems of James Reaney,* Thomas Gerry explores the emblems, both published and unpublished. Each one is illuminated by its setting among other closely-related Reaney poems and plays, by the poet's intellectual debts to Blake, Jung, and Frye, and by his practices as a visual artist. Reaney's erudition is matched by Gerry's investigation of the ancient emblem tradition, and his sensitivity to the central motive of Reaney's multifaceted creative life: to challenge us to perceive actively, magnetically. In doing so Gerry unveils the resources of one of the richest texts in Canadian poetry. — Germaine Warkentin

We learn to draw (scrawls, squiggles, a person, a house) before we learn to read or write. It was characteristic of James Reaney in mid-career to produce his emblem poems, thereby not only joining a long tradition but also illustrating (also with scrawls, squiggles, and various more identifiable images) the main preoccupations of his poetry, plays, libretti, and paintings — the basics of his art, in effect. Thomas Gerry has performed an original exercise in brilliantly examining the ten emblems in relation to specific Reaney works in other forms. His observations are meticulous and wide-ranging, and they illuminate Reaney's oeuvre in new and fundamental ways. In particular, I appreciate his citations from Rhoda Kellogg's studies of children's art (known to Reaney) and I find it refreshing that he deals at length with Reaney's activities as an opera librettist, seldom touched on by other commentators. — John Beckwith

The Emblems of James Reaney

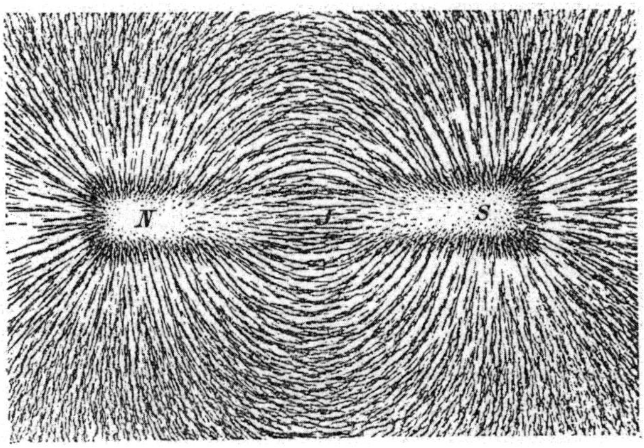

MAGNETICALLY DRAWN

Thomas Gerry

The Porcupine's Quill

Library and Archives Canada Cataloguing in Publication

Gerry, Thomas Martin Farr, 1948–
The emblems of James Reaney: magnetically drawn / Thomas Gerry.

Includes bibliographical references and index.
ISBN 978-0-88984-358-5

1. Reaney, James, 1926–2008 —- Criticism and interpretation.
2. Emblems in literature. I. Title. II. Title: Magnetically drawn.

PS8535.E24Z68 2013 C818'.5409 C2013-900523-4

1 2 3 4 • 15 14 13

Published by The Porcupine's Quill, 68 Main Street, PO Box 160,
Erin, Ontario NOB 1TO. http://porcupinesquill.ca

Readied for the press by Tom Smart.

Represented in Canada by the Literary Press Group.
Trade orders are available from University of Toronto Press.

We acknowledge the support of the Ontario Arts Council and the Canada Council for the Arts for our publishing program. The financial support of the Government of Canada through the Canada Book Fund is also gratefully acknowledged.

Canada

Ontario
Ontario Media Development Corporation

Canada Council for the Arts
Conseil des Arts du Canada

ONTARIO ARTS COUNCIL
CONSEIL DES ARTS DE L'ONTARIO

To Linda,
with love and thanks

Table of Contents

Introduction

Man is man's ABC: there is none that can
Reade God aright, unless he first spell Man....
— Francis Quarles, *Hieroglyphike* 1, 1638

A challenge facing anyone who attempts to articulate the meanings of James Reaney's work is that so much is involved, even though the work itself at first might seem uncomplicated. In some 'Production Notes' for *Listen to the Wind,* Reaney observes that 'The simpler art is, the richer it is' (141). This maxim certainly applies to his emblems. While his creations are based on his sophisticated understanding of English culture from the Renaissance to the Modern period, as well as his encyclopaedic knowledge of Ontario's culture, nevertheless Reaney's writing and artwork are in some ways child-like: they toy with words and images, and draw audiences and readers into their playful worlds. His entire book of *Performance Poems* (1990) is prefaced with an ostensibly casual invitation to 'try out these new pieces as a way of giving groups of people an experience of poetry's power to reach out and focus an audience that may have long forgotten how nursery rhymes and street games stir up the soul with the joy of unifying so many of the senses, so many of your friend-circle' (3). The meaning of the pieces, Reaney suggests, is the shared experience of remembering and finding joy. The phrase 'groups of people' highlights his wish to bring performers and audiences together into community. Individually, remembering in some depth calls for research, depending on one's level of curiosity, and the efficiency of one's memory; just who is this 'Sir Charles Goddam Roberts' (8) anyway?[1] Reaney's elaboration of the joyful experiences of poetry as 'unifying so many of the senses', also suggests why he inclines to multi-sensory, multi-art creation, such as emblems, plays and opera, with their texts, images and sounds.

'Bringing people together around poems that stir up the soul with joy' is an apt way to state Reaney's understanding of the poet's role. As he passionately emphasized in 'Vision in Canada', a 2001 article, the poet's function is important and letting it work is urgent:

> Outer space — money galore for it: but for inner space, the secrets behind actually getting people to love each other, to prevent Macbeth and Lady Macbeth getting into our schools and shooting the scholars, very few successes there. The Bible is in trouble, the Church is in trouble, mathematics cannot produce a more loving society, neither can the system that, if you're mentally ill, responds with a pill. What has gone wrong with visions and stories that used to work? (940)

With his poems, plays, fiction, essays and emblems, Reaney does create visions and stories that 'work'. He observes later in the same article: 'Unlock the mind-forged manacles and the infant will stop crying with fear and the soldier sighing as his blood no longer runs down palace walls — to paraphrase Blake' (944).

Northrop Frye, in his masterful literary study *Fearful Symmetry,* also refers to the English Romantic poet William Blake to explain the poet's social function. I quote at some length here because the ideas are fundamental to Reaney's art too (as echoes of the above statements by Reaney indicate).[2]

> Cosmology is a literary art, but there are two kinds of cosmology, the kind designed to understand the world as it is, and the kind designed to transform it into the form of human desire. Platonists and occultists deal with the former kind, which after Newton's time, according to Blake, became the accepted form of science. Cosmology of this type is speculative, which, as the etymology of that word shows, is ultimately intellectual narcissism, staring into nature as the mirror of our ordinary selves. What the mirror shows us is what Blake calls 'mathematic form', the automatic and mindless universe that has no beginning nor end, no up nor down. What such a universe suggests to us is resignation, acceptance of what is predictable, fear of whatever is unpredictable. Blake's cosmology, of which the symbol is Ezekiel's vision of the chariot of God with its

> 'wheels within wheels', is a revolutionary vision of the universe transformed by the creative imagination into a human shape. This cosmology is not speculative but concerned, not reactionary but revolutionary, not a vision of things as they are ordered but of things as they could be ordered. (n.p.)

This book's intent is to show ways in which Reaney's emblems and other works venture to transform the universe into human shape, or to make his readers understand that, as Francis Quarles puts it, 'Man is man's ABC'.

Before focusing on the emblems, it will be useful to understand Reaney's artistic practice, which is closely related to emblematic thinking — the use of wit in particular. This background, I hope, will create a greater appreciation of exactly why his emblems are fundamental to his work as a whole.

---

1. A Canlit 'joke' that mocks the aristocratic pretentiousness of the person whom some people call 'the Father of Canadian poetry', Sir Charles G.D. Roberts. He was born in Douglas, New Brunswick, in 1860, and died in 1943, with many honours, including a knighthood (conferred in 1935). John Coldwell Adams published a biography of him, with the title *Sir Charles God Damn: The Life of Sir Charles G.D. Roberts.* (Toronto: University of Toronto Press, 1986).

2. The reader will notice that this book relies heavily on Northrop Frye's understanding of William Blake. This reliance is not only because of the clarity and depth of Frye's writings, but also because they were the main lens through which Reaney viewed Blake. Richard Stingle's article gives a thorough account of the development of Reaney's understanding of Frye's ideas.

A Brief History of Emblems

Although we now might use the term 'emblem' loosely as a synonym for 'symbol' or 'insignia', emblems are actually a distinct form of literature. The word 'emblem' derives from the Greek term for an 'insertion' (ἔμβλημα), which became '*emblema*' in Latin, meaning decorative inlaid work or a raised ornament on a vessel. A literary emblem consists of a picture accompanied by a motto — a Greek or Latin quotation, commonly, or a passage from the Bible — and an explanatory text, often in verse. In emblems, the words and images interpret each other, and most often the interpretation is a moral lesson. Books of emblems were especially popular in Europe in the sixteenth and seventeenth centuries. Mario Praz explains in his study of seventeenth-century imagery that they were 'a humanistic attempt to give a modern equivalent of the [Egyptian] hieroglyphs' (23).

Attempts to reconcile classical — pagan — philosophy with Christian humanist doctrine were made over a long period beginning with the teachings of Clement of Alexandria (d. c. 215), his pupil Origen (c. 185–254), and St. Augustine (354–430). This integration spread throughout Christendom a millennium later, during the Renaissance, largely emanating from the Florentine philosopher Marsilio Ficino's translations and commentaries on classical works. Ficino (1433–1499) believed in the reunion of heaven and earth in the souls of human beings. Echoing Plato's teaching in the *Timaeus,* Ficino stated that each individual has an immortal soul; therefore, he reasoned, human beings have access by direct experience to the divine. Ficino's teachings on human spiritual development involved people's furthering their understanding through contemplation of natural events and things *as symbolical:* not only the sun, the motions of stars and planets, animals and plants, the human body, and so on, but also music and visual images symbolize spiritual truths. Such contemplation, Ficino taught, could lead people to experience oneness with the divine directly, not exclusively through the intercession of priests.

Dum aetatis ver agitur: consule brumae
In winter coulde, when tree, and bushe, was bare,
and frost had nip'd the rootes of tender grasse:
The antes, with joye did feede upon their fare,
Which they had stor'de, while sommers season was:
To whome, for foode the grashopper did crie,
And said she starv'd, if they did helpe denie.
Whereat, an ante, with longe experience wise?
And frost, and snowe, had manie winters seene:
Inquired, what in sommer was her guise.

— Geffrey Whitney, *A Choice of Emblemes* (159)

Writers soon began to claim this power for words too. New translations of the Bible into vernacular languages and the wide distribution of these sacred books, thanks to the printing press, gave substance to the writers' claim. In his study of *ekphrasis,* Murray Krieger presents a history of how words and images from the Middle Ages to the Renaissance vied with each other for supremacy as sign systems. In summary, he writes,

> Once the shift from natural-sign picture to picture-as-code has occurred, it is a short step to a configuration of words that would turn themselves into a form that is the self-enclosed equivalent of an emblem, in effect a verbal emblem. The visual emblem and the verbal emblem are complementary languages for seeking the representation of the unrepresentable. (22)

The visual arts predominated, however, being, as Plato had argued, more natural signs than language, which is further removed from the ideal forms. The aim of language use was to emulate the virtues of painting. For example, one of the key terms used by critics to assess verbal works was 'enargeia' — from the Greek ἔναργης meaning 'visible, palpable, manifest' — a word which Aristotle used in discussing effective oratory. In literature, enargeia is the rhetorical accomplishment of describing things so vividly that they 'appear' in the mind's eye.

As well as being part of the Renaissance project of reconciling Egyptian and classical thought with Christianity, and as educational tools to share Christian doctrine, on a more practical level emblem books were popular because the newly invented printing presses produced them effectively. The first emblem book was published in 1531: the Italian lawyer Andrea Alciato's *Emblematum Liber.*[1] With *A Choice of Emblemes,* Geffrey Whitney's translations of some of these European texts, along with reproductions of the accompanying illustrations, emblems began to be published in English in 1586. One important shift in the composition of emblems when they appeared in England is summarized by the scholar Roger Sharrock:

> While Alciati and the early continental emblematists were courtly and literary in tone, their English followers, Whitney, Quarles and Wither, were pious and popular, and therefore, being English, militantly Protestant. (106)

In her authoritative appraisal of English emblems, Rosemary Freeman points out that emblems indicate a way of thinking, the allegorical: the sense that everything has a dual meaning.

> In the reign of Elizabeth allegory was still an essential part of life, as it had been, only more profoundly, in the Middle Ages. Its basis was social: it entered into the occupations of every day. The accounts of the progresses of the Queen represent an England in which nothing had a single meaning and nothing lacked significance.... Nor had allegory its province only at Court.... Colour and decoration, gesture and action had a double meaning which was everywhere emphasized. (1–2)

Freeman explains that allegory became 'less public and more psychological' with the passing of the century, 1586–1686, during which emblem books flourished:

> The material of *The Faerie Queene* is derived in part from the social life of the Court, from its tournaments, its ceremonial, its setting. The personified figures which Spenser uses so frequently might be found painted on a ceiling, embroidered on a cloak, or woven in a tapestry; but the material of Herbert's *Temple* is to be found in the human heart. The same individual sense of the dual meaning of things continues, but the interest has turned inward. (2)

As an example of this inwardness, Freeman quotes Elizabeth Grymeston's 1604 *Miscelanea*:

> Canst thou feele the wind beat on thy face, and canst thou forget that thou holdest thy tenement by a puffe of winde? canst thou sit by the river side, and not remember that as the river runneth, and doth not returne, so is the life of man? (2)

Freeman notes that 'the last coherent formulation of this way of thinking' is Bunyan's *Pilgrim's Progress* (2), and speculates that the rise of science, with its relentless search for causes and effects, was largely responsible for the eclipse of allegorical thought.

A final background detail from Freeman's book is helpful for understanding why Elizabethans loved emblems so much. Freeman says that in addition to being fashionable, 'a gentlemanly accomplishment of the same type as the ability to play the lute or to dance the lavolta', emblem writing was a result of 'the recurrent and restless desire in human nature to exercise the power of reason . . .'. She goes on:

> What was primarily emphasized in the emblem fashion by those who defended it was its 'wit'; and, although the intelligence required to perceive that wit may not have been of a particularly high order, the man who had successfully followed the emblem writer through his exposition of the connection between a symbol and its significance was left with the same pleasant assurance that his reason had not been allowed to fust in him unused as is the man who today follows the oblique approach of an advertiser to his subject or guesses a clue in a crossword puzzle. For both, it is the wit, the apparent lack of any relation between two ideas and the subsequent establishment of an intellectually convincing link between them, that pleases; it does not matter how forced and arbitrary the link may seem to common-sense or feeling. (3)

After perusing several books of emblems such as Whitney's (see page 14), I have to say that at least for this reader, considerably more assurance of my own rationality derives from appreciating the links among the elements of emblems than from figuring out the connections between famous skaters and toothpaste, say, or the clue, 'transport a wild animal', and 'bear'. Still, the mental activity — not entirely rational, either — is the point here. Reaney is well-known as a teacher, poet and dramatist in the Blakean tradition, and faculty rousing has always been one of his primary concerns. As he put it in 1991: 'we cannot have enough art that seeks to wake up people and get them in touch with their identities through its theatricality' (*Gale* 308).

---

1. The name appears both as 'Alciati' and 'Alciato'. In addition to the standard print sources on the subject of emblem books, such as Bath, Daly's *English Emblem*, Freeman, Green and Praz, there is a useful internet site on Alciato: http://www.mun.ca/alciato/index.html.

Reaney's Visionary Method

The Play-Box

In his Author's Note to *Colours in the Dark,* Reaney suggests that *Colours* 'might best be called a play box', which, like his own, is 'filled with not only toys and school relics, but also deedboxes, ancestral coffin plates — in short, a whole life' (7). Once he makes this leap from actual things to what they bring to mind ('a whole life'), Reaney underscores the active role expected from his readers and playgoing audiences:

> The theatrical experience in front of you now is designed to give you that mosaic — that all-things happening-at-the-same-time-galaxy-higgledy-piggledy feeling that rummaging through a play box can give you. (7)

So *Colours in the Dark,* as with all of Reaney's creations, is not designed to convey a particular abstract meaning, but instead to create a living feeling that involves everyone present, a feeling that puts events and facts and particularly the people themselves in a new light. Reaney is creating communities by getting people to take part, not by describing them. It is in this sense primarily that his work is local, not so much that it documents nearby people and places.

What *is* the feeling that is the meaning of his plays? The actor Jerry Franken puts it eloquently in his Afterword to Reaney's *Performance Poems.* Franken describes the similarity in two different experiences of reciting lines from Reaney's play *Handcuffs,* one on stage in unison with two other actors, the other in a university classroom with twelve students. Franken says that 'despite the difference, the *feeling* was the same, a kind of exhilaration brought on by becoming one with the word together' (104). Reaney expresses a more specific take on this feeling: 'Surely one of the things theatre could be about is the relaxed awareness that comes when you simply play' (8). Again paradoxically, this active play is anything but 'foolish', as we might understand the term, as being in opposition to the seriousness of work. Playing, though, transforms our mundane lives from what he calls 'the Age of Dread' (8) into 'a peaceable kingdom — energetic, joyful and serene,' ... making 'the world of dread much easier to face afterwards' (9).

Germaine Warkentin, a most perceptive critic and the editor of Reaney's *Poems,* calls transformation the 'single structural principle common to all Reaney's creative thought'. She suggests that transformations in Reaney's works are a kind of translation 'in which the identity of seemingly unlike things is unexpectedly revealed and they are transformed from the voiceless chaos of human experience into the eloquence of metaphor' (*Poems* viii). For example, this process is enacted by the play-box objects' metamorphosing into 'a whole life'. And the process results in the 'new light' I mentioned, caused by the 'living feeling' that is the meaning of Reaney's works.

The transformative process involves turning our assumptions upside down and inside out because most of us are caught in the net of our cultures' scientific 'understanding', which Frye noted, as opposed to the 'revolutionary' approach that strives for transformation of the world in which we exist. As a result, if we the audience are stuck in the Age of Dread, Reaney's work could seem obscure and, well, dreadful. But his work is asking us to see with new eyes.

How does Reaney accomplish these transformations? In short, his technique is to juxtapose elements of the Age-of-Dread world — history and documentary — as one magnetic pole, while the other pole is elements from myths and dreams, the world as we'd like it to be. The interactions of these polar elements creates a transformation, a sense of seeing the world anew.

To begin to explore the development of this method, let's look again at the play-box image, already discussed with reference to *Colours in the Dark.* In an early poem called 'Play-box' (*Poems* 5), the young speaker is frightened of being orphaned, and imagines, should his step-father die, a way of life alternative to his ordinary, dreary farming existence. The two magnetic poles are thus established. The child's new (imaginary) life of camping 'in a fence-corner' and being 'independent awhile', involves his taking with him things like his 'spotted ring' and his play-box with its 'old toys and scrap-books. And poor dead butterfly wings.' These things are images to be renewed through loving attention, similarly to how the play-box, as the butterfly wings suggest, becomes a cocoon for the speaker's transformative renewal in time with seasonal changes:

> I shall shut myself up in my play-box hall.
> Shut the lid; sleep the winter through.
> With my toy green lantern for light.
> They'll find me in the spring.

The mention of the ring and the green lantern invokes the magical changes featured in *Green Lantern* comics, which began publication in 1940, and were apt reading for this boy who has decided to suspend the threatening workaday world, the Age of Dread, in favour of playfully inhabiting Nature's rhythms, and dreaming his way to a 'possible home'.

Reaney's later poem 'The Butterfly and the Moth' (1961) reveals the influences of Frye and Blake in its refinement of the transformative pattern. Insisting on a change in perspective, the poem's title appears right side up on the page, and the text of the poem is upside down. The poem's speaker describes his condition of wintry death ('bonfires' standing for his senses); then he expresses a vague hope:

> The Earth, that huge & dirty Lout,
> Has my five bonfires all put out....
>
> Alas, beneath the drifts of snow
> No greens for caterpillars grow.
> I'll build of nothing and of sorrow
> From ashes and of autumn dust
> A cradle coffin ark which must
> Somehow float me to tomorrow.

While the word 'Somehow' indicates an enduring mystery, the list-like phrasing and implicit identifying of 'cradle coffin ark' suggest that no matter how dead its materials, poetic creativity — turning chaos into metaphor, as Warkentin put it — is able to stimulate new life.

When the speaker's metamorphosis does occur, Nature again is central, but not undifferentiated Nature, as in 'Play-Box'. Natural images, such as the Earth in the poem's first part, convey the speaker's sense of death; in the second part of the poem, natural images nourish the speaker back to life. Consistent with Blake's cosmology, this refinement in the roles of Nature images between the two poems shows an increase in emphasis on the psychic, internal changes required of the speaker in 'The Butterfly and the Moth', and decreases the emphasis on the external act of simply entrusting human changes to Nature's powers, as presented in 'Play-Box'. Here is the last verse paragraph of 'The Butterfly and the Moth':

In my dead hands grows a fine grass,
The waste fork sprouts a mushroom.
In my eyes come the Sun & the Moon.
I hear again the South Wind pass.
In my nails rise rain white clouds.
My empty head teems flower crowds,
And sing to me a Butterfly
Who wise & reckless passes by
The tight closed flowers of death and doth
Leave them for the brown winged moth. (*Poems* 189)

By contrasting the totally human characterization of the butterfly as life-bringing, probably because of its bright colours and daytime activities, while characterizing the nocturnal, brown moth as a death symbol, the final five lines here sum up this more complex approach. As compared with the 'Play-Box', here Nature is both death-bringer and life-giver, according to the speaker's vision. The poem insists on the human speaker's 'inner' psychological role in his death-to-life transformation, in this case, the speaker's assigning symbolic valuations to butterfly and moth, and writing a poem about it.

Reaney's artistic vision is remarkably consistent throughout his career. The 'Play-Box' poem is dated 1945 in Warkentin's edition. At about the age of nineteen, or before, he understood that for him to develop as an artist it was essential that he get out of himself, and he was actively looking for ways out. The technique he developed is certainly

Apollonian, in that it is a fully conscious activity. As an undergraduate at the University of Toronto, he expressed the need for a system to organize his 'notebooks filled with metaphors', as he called his writing; 'what I wanted to know was — what backbones and what galaxies do these lists belong to and in.... [A]lready I was conscious of needing the patterns for longer poems than lyrics' ('Identifier' 27).

At this early point in his career, wanting to leave behind lyrical self-expression and instead move towards creating art with a more ambitious, transformative aim, Reaney proceeded inductively: from the particular metaphors in his notebooks towards general categories. This method involved organizing his metaphors in the contexts of various traditional texts, ranging from local lore to comic books to world mythologies. Many poets and artists have taken this step of finding 'backbones' for their personal observations. Reaney did, however, largely abandon the lyric for writing plays. The achievement that sets his work apart is that he performed in the open, alone and with others, this bringing together of materials and structures for the purpose not of self-expression, but of social transformation.

Wit

Reaney explicitly articulates the development of his artistic method in the pages of the journal *Alphabet*, which he produced from 1960 to 1971.[1] This method involves the use of wit, a term more common and more precisely defined in the fifteenth and sixteenth centuries than it is now. Rosemary Freeman describes the practice of wit in her study of early English emblems as 'the apparent lack of any relation between two ideas and the subsequent establishment of an intellectually convincing link between them'(3). As the core method of *Alphabet*, devoted to studying the 'iconography of the imagination', Reaney was using wit, but expressing it metaphorically. Here is how he states the method in the first issue of *Alphabet*:

> Let us make a form out of this: documentary on one side and myth on the other: Life and Art. In this form we can put anything and the magnet we have set up will arrange it for us. (3)

Whether or not Reaney was stimulated to use the magnet metaphor because of its appearance in Edward Kleiman's story 'Crystal Pillow' (59) in this same first issue of *Alphabet,* the magnetic becomes *Alphabet's* method, as well as the method of most of Reaney's works. In each issue documentary material, usually an essay or essays, is brought together with mythic material. Presiding over such magnetic poles in each issue is an iconographic figure. The first issue, for instance, is governed by the Tarot deck's Fool (82). Issue 1 presents the first part of Jay Macpherson's essay called 'Narcissus: Some Uncertain Reflections', which, even with its clever, wittily punning title, is actually a scholarly exploration of the Narcissus figure. Juxtaposed as a magnetic pole for this documentary piece are several stories and poems, including 'Crystal Pillow'.

In the editorial which opens the second issue of *Alphabet,* Reaney muses about some features of the first issue which were 'unanticipated'. In rereading the material in issue 1, he writes, he noticed a pattern of mirrors: in the Narcissus essay by Macpherson, for instance; in the 'form' Reaney proposes for *Alphabet:* 'documentary on one side and myth on the other: Life and Art'; in the image of the 'crystal pillow' in the story of that name; even, perhaps, in the layout of his own poem, 'The Alphabet', which is centre-justified on the page, thereby suggesting a pattern of one side's reflecting the other; and certainly the mirror is present in the formidable task of Reaney's hand-setting the magazine in type. In the second issue, the 'unanticipated' pattern that emerges is childhood. Reaney attributes these emergences of mirrors and childhood to the magnet form of *Alphabet.* He says that by polarizing documentary and legend as opposite ends of a magnet, 'In each case the legend takes something from the many thousand somethings of the child's world and gives it a meaning, makes it part of a design.' For Reaney, giving something a meaning involves perceiving it as part of a larger pattern. This perception involves the wit inherent in allegorical, emblematic thinking.

Reaney's Education and the English Protestant Emblem Tradition

An inclination to emblematic thought extends also to Reaney's reading. Over the years he studied and used as models for his own writings, works from the Elizabethan period and earlier. Even as a child, he has noted on several occasions, he was influenced by the works of the seventeenth-century allegorist and emblematist John Bunyan. Asked in 1996 by Wanda Campbell of the *University of Windsor Review* just where his 'fascination with the verbal universe' began, Reaney replied: 'It was the Bible, and being raised among people who were interested in theatre in a country farm setting with a library that had *Pilgrim's Progress* in it and religious books on the apocalypse' (11).

From Reaney's entry in the *Gale Contemporary Authors Autobiography Series,* we learn that he had started to create emblems at least as early as 1944 to 1948, during his undergraduate years at University College, University of Toronto. Reflecting on the Toronto poet's predicament, he writes:

> In one of my orange Coil-Rotary notebooks from this period I have an emblematic drawing called 'Queen Street' in which a vista down to the Don Jail, symbolized by a gallows, is framed by a young rolled-stocking woman on stage right and a randy, vigorous old tramp as her opposite, sinister companion. Between them, some red lanterns guard an excavation in which the body of a suicide poet has been discovered. (15)

Fortunately, after receiving his MA in 1949, Reaney was hired to teach at the University of Manitoba, so he escaped any such dire, if picturesque, fate.[2] In 1956, nevertheless, he returned to the University of Toronto for doctoral work, both to become a qualified university professor, and 'to become more expert in literary symbolism, structure and genre' (*Gale* 15).

As a doctoral student, Reaney took, among other courses, Northrop Frye's 'Literary Symbolism', which 'was soon to appear as a book called *Anatomy of Criticism* ('Identifier' 29). One of the key arguments of *Anatomy* is that literature is not just a 'piled aggregate of "works", but an order of words' (17). *Anatomy of Criticism* undertakes to elaborate this 'backbone' of literature.

Reaney's doctoral thesis, supervised by Frye, among others, is a study of Edmund Spenser's influence on the work of William Butler Yeats. Somewhat audaciously for a young student's work, the thesis traces the way Yeats's poetry and plays improve as he moves away from his early misinterpretation of Spenser, caused by his failure to perceive the symbolic structures of the Renaissance poet's works. Reaney's summary of Yeats's (and others') blindness is instructive because it precisely defines allegorical, emblematic thinking:

> Yeats, his contemporaries and his immediate poetic forebears have lost the power poets still had in Spenser's day to 'consider all things in the world', as Yeats says later on, 'as a dictionary of types and symbols', that is, they have lost the power to see the universe as the content of the poet's mind.... ('Influence' 18)

Heroically, according to Reaney, Yeats regained this power, abandoning the beautiful *symboliste* surfaces of his early work. An important feature of this transformation is Yeats's rejection of the continental Catholic view of salvation in favour of the British Protestant view. In discussing these divergent interpretations, Reaney focuses on differences in poetic voices:

> Do they speak directly to us, or do they turn their backs on us? Do they speak in cultured highbrow tones as from a great height, or do they seem to think there is some hope that we will understand.... Finally do they side with T.E. Hulme in regarding man as a limited bucket, or do they think that man is a limitless giant in power who may be asleep but is slowly rousing himself? The alternatives in each question are the alternatives between a popular English, Protestant and revolutionary tradition and an esoteric, French-inspired, Catholic and conservative one. ('Influence' 234)

The importance of this formulation, in terms of Reaney's work as an emblematist, is the clarity of his valorizing the 'popular English, Protestant and revolutionary tradition' — precisely the tradition out of which grew the Renaissance English emblem books, and in which Reaney himself was raised.[3] His concern with community, noted in the Introduction (page 9), is rooted also in this democratic and revolutionary 'hope that we will understand'. Also crucially, as Reaney puts it, the doctoral work informed by *Fearful Symmetry*, Frye's lectures, the Spenser-Yeats thesis, and *Anatomy of Criticism* 'opened out the verbal universe for me' ('Identifier' 29–30). In other words, Reaney's path was similar to Yeats's in that both poets gained the power 'to see the universe as the content of the poet's mind'. In his early study of Reaney, Ross Woodman notes this milestone by characterizing Reaney with Frye's epithet for Blake: he had become a 'literalist of the imagination' (14). It is worth noting too that the practice of psychoanalysis resembles the creation of artwork: transforming the world, including the 'inner world', into words, substantiates the world as given to us, and makes it human.

Spenser's *Faerie Queene,* as Freeman observes, is part of the early 'public' phase of allegorical writing (see page 16), whereas Bunyan's *Pilgrim's Progress* is more psychologically oriented. In his study '*The Pilgrim's Progress* and Allegory', Brian Nellist argues that

> It is this placing of all significance in the interior processes of the hero which most sharply distinguishes [*Pilgrim's Progress*] from earlier allegory. Spenser's knights, for example, are shadowy creatures because they exist only to meet further segmentations of a way of life of which they are merely the central image.... But in Bunyan it is not so much what the hero sees that matters as his response to it and what he is in himself. (134)

Spenser and Bunyan are clear inflences, both in Reaney's work of the period that led up to the publication of his emblem poems and, equally, in the work that came after. Spenser's *Shepheardes Calender* (1579) is the source of the dialogue format, and the 'fables, sestinas, singing matches, the passage of a year' (Poems 145), as well as many themes in Reaney's 1958 book *A Suit of Nettles.* Also like Spenser's *Shepheardes Calender* and *The Pilgrim's Progress, A Suit of Nettles* is annotated by the author. The *Shepheardes Calender* contains emblematic woodcuts at the beginning of each month's section, suggesting the appropriateness of illustrating such a work. The 2010 edition of *A Suit of Nettles* similarly contains illustrations.

Reaney's poem 'A Cellar Song', published in 1959, is a mini-catalogue of typical basement items using names similar to those found in *Pilgrim's Progress* and in the symbolic masques which preceded it. Here are the opening lines of 'A Cellar Song':

> There's just ourselves
> On these dusty shelves

Master Jug and Mistress Pitcher
Sister Cistern
Cobweb Bottle
Sarah Sowbeetle
Potato Sprout and
Milly Moon.... (380)

The poem's 'action' is generated vertically, with wit, by contemplation of the personifications and the names' meanings in relation to each other, rather than by the more modern means of characters' interactions based on a plot. Bunyan did write an illustrated emblem book (*A Book for Boys and Girls*, 1686), but *Pilgrim's Progress* was not pictorially illustrated. The book does contain many word emblems, though, similar to Reaney's 'The Red Heart', especially in the Interpreter's House section. Here is an excerpt from the word emblem of Despair. (In the margin is the explanatory note: *'Despair like an Iron Cage'*.)

> So [the Interpreter] took [Christian] by the hand again, and led him into a very dark Room, where there sat a man in an Iron Cage.
>
> Now the Man, to look on, seemed very sad: he sat with his eyes looking down to the ground, his hands folded together; and he sighed as if he would break his heart. Then said *Christian, What means this?* At which the *Interpreter* bid him talk with the Man.
>
> Then said *Christian* to the Man, *What art thou?* The Man answered, *I am what I once was not....* I am *now* a Man of Despair, and am shut up in it, as in this Iron Cage. I cannot get out; O *now* I cannot. (34)

In part, this word emblem is an example of *ekphrasis*. Its evocation of a picture, though, is multi-dimensional in that it leads to the moral that despair is sinful because it leads to a dead end. Many critics and commentators have attempted to establish exactly which pictorial emblems Bunyan was putting into words. The man in the iron cage, Sharrock argues, for example, is probably based on Quarles' *Emblemes*, Book V, number 10, 'where the illustration shows a man in a cage with an angel outside'; below it on the page is a verse from the fourteenth Psalm, 'Bring my Soule out of Prison ...' (111–12). Sharrock ignores the fact that Psalm 14 begins, as he quotes it, 'My Soul is like a Bird, my flesh the cage' (112). Anyway, rather than get further entangled in these details, I will simply emphasize again the emblematic way of thinking on multiple levels at once, even in non-illustrated material, with which Reaney was deeply familiar. From here it would not have been a long step to Reaney's creating his own emblems incorporating pictures as well as words.

'Metaphor is reality'

For a further understanding of Reaney's emblem making, it is important to distinguish his emblems, based in the Protestant English emblem tradition, from the earlier tradition. In medieval times, as Freeman explains, 'the whole world had been symbolic, and all the details of experience had formed part of one unified conception of the meaning of life' (20). For the Elizabethans, she claims, 'this great framework no longer existed as a single unity' (20), so the emblem writers had to point out the symbolic meanings and their moral implications, as Bunyan does in his *Divine Emblems: or Temporal Things Spiritualized. Fitted for the Use of Boys and Girls.* For the twentieth-century emblematist, living in a culture permeated by utilitarian scientific values that distort the ancient hierarchical concepts, a revised approach is also inevitable. Reaney's emblems call attention to allegorical and symbolic dimensions of life in order to rouse the readers' faculties anew, to encourage and enable them to perceive their worlds more richly — to realize that a circle, rectangle and triangle are more than mere shapes, that trees are more than trade items. One of Reaney's earliest statements of this purpose is in his Editorial for the first issue of *Alphabet*, in 1960:

> I can remember about twelve years ago at Toronto feeling the final clutch of the so-called scientific world. Metaphors seemed lies. Poetry seemed to have no use at all. The moon looked enchanting through the trees on Charles Street, but the enchantment was really nothing but an illusion of clouds and fantasy covering up a hideous pock-marked spherical desert. When I told this part of my problem to a friend, whose work appears in this issue, he showed me a passage from the *Marriage of Heaven and Hell* which had the

> effect of starting me back to the belief I had held as a young child that metaphor is reality.... Those were the months when young men and women sat up all night reading *Fearful Symmetry* which had just come out. I think I have been present at more conversations about the Fall than even Adam could have thrown a certain withered apple core at, and assuredly more speculations concerning Leviathan than Job scratched his boils to. Here in your hands lies one of the effects of those conversations — a small secret looking book devoted to the proposition that it is very interesting mankind should answer the terrors of the inner and the outer world with a symbolic fruit and an iconic sea-beast. Interest increases with exploration. This attitude is to me one of the most stimulating areas of intellectual life in Canada. A traveller from abroad would immediately pick it out. *Ils ont parlé toute la nuit de baleines blanches!* (3–4)

Reaney's explanation of his interest in symbolism makes evident again the importance he places on the social aspect of the arts. (Publishing a magazine is itself a social project, of course.) His concerns are with the community's awakening as well as with the individual's. Secondly, his belief that 'metaphor is reality' could be the motto for the study of Reaney's emblems. They dramatize this very proposition. Readers/interpreters therefore find themselves at the centre of the emblem process.

An example of Reaney's emblematic thinking in action outside of his emblem book chapters is *Twelve Letters to a Small Town,* an illustrated book he published in 1961, which was set to music by John Beckwith.

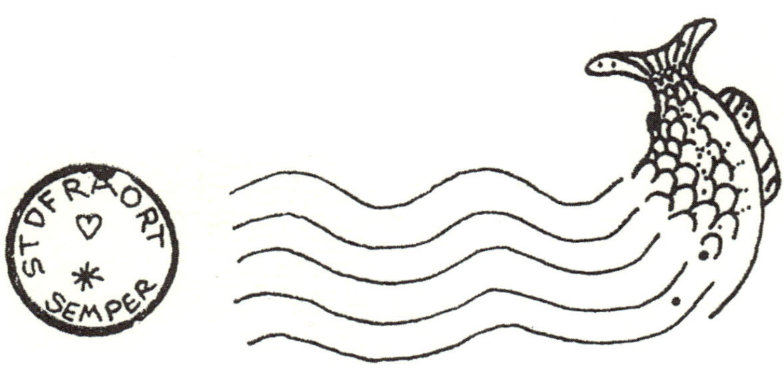

Twelve Letters' theme is the growth of a young Canadian poet of the 1930s and '40s, who is uncomfortably conscious of the clash between the English cultural heritage so fervently celebrated with names, events and attitudes in his hometown, Stratford, Ontario, and the physical fact of his being in Canada. The series of letters dramatizes the process of the poet's becoming individually aware of this disjunction and then arriving at a broader social vision, expressed metaphorically, of how the two apparently incongruous circumstances can actually function creatively and harmoniously.

The visual illustrations in *Twelve Letters* are not strictly emblems, although there are similarities; they are fanciful drawings that complement the text by suggesting transformation through postal themes and images of movement. The closest that *Twelve Letters* gets to presenting an emblem is all words, in the First Letter, the often-anthologized 'To the Avon River above Stratford, Canada'. Having rejected the river's English name 'the Avon' as inappropriate, the poet yet does not know its name, but is able to imagine for the river a coat of arms with a motto:

> A shield of reeds and cresses
>   Sedges, crayfishes
> The hermaphroditic leech
> Minnows, muskrats and farmers' geese
> And printed above this shield
> One of my earliest wishes
> 'To flow like you.'
>
> From *Letters to a Small Town* (*Poems* 212)

The imagined design on the shield is a list of plants and animals found in and near the river. These verbal images devised and assigned by the poet stand for the river more accurately than the name 'Avon'. At the same time, the images taken together form a synecdoche — a type of metaphor in which parts stand for a whole — the plants and animals representing the river without actually naming it. The shield's motto, 'To flow like you', is the poet's wish to be transformed into the person he already is, not defined by imposed names and terms, but by his own language.

Subsequent letters in this sequence reach out to the small town's buildings and streets, people, history and institutions, enlarging the scope of the longed-for transformation and hence the poet's social role. This pattern of expanding spheres of transformation in *Twelve Letters* is correlated to the twelve stages of the alchemical process of changing leaden matter into spiritual gold, as Wanda Campbell elaborates in her article on 'Alchemy in Ontario'. Reaney had read C.G. Jung's book *Psychology and Alchemy,* and had used it extensively in his thesis on Spenser and Yeats. *Psychology and Alchemy* also informs many of Reaney's emblems, in both their forms and their themes. In adapting the alchemical process as a literary structure, Reaney is not just taking part in people's age-old habit of retelling stories. His project is rather to bring about spiritual renewal through his work. In *Twelve Letters,* the procedure is to challenge the British literary tradition in the Canadian setting through imaginative language and pictures. His emblems intensively involve readers/viewers in the 'projection of psychic contents', in Jung's terms. Attempting to elucidate the often arcane theory of the alchemists — theory which Reaney adapted for his parallel purposes — Jung quotes Julius Evola's *La Tradizione Ermetica* (1931):

> The spiritual condition of man in the premodern cycles of culture was such that each physical perception had simultaneously a psychic component which 'animated' it, adding a 'significance' to the bare image, and at the same time a special and potent emotional tone. Thus the ancient physics was both a theology and a transcendental psychology, by reason of the illuminating flashes from metaphysical essences which penetrated through the matter of the bodily senses. Natural science was at once a spiritual science, and the many meanings of the symbols united under the various aspects of a single knowledge. (Jung *Psychology* 231)

As a literary and visual artist, and as a musician, Reaney has always been fascinated by multiple meanings, and techniques to achieve multidimensionality in his work. Richard Stingle, for instance, quotes Reaney's explanation of his enthusiastic discovery of literary analogies to musical counterpoint:

> Once I absorbed both Frye and Blake on 'Poetry is allegory addressed to the intellectual powers' what happened was that I was

> finally able to stand in the house of literature and close the door on philosophy, theology and history until I needed them. In short, you can explain literature in terms of itself, something that is so obvious in mathematics and music, but seemed so difficult in my first years at Toronto. When I was in my last year at high school, I can remember reading in my Counterpoint textbook that its system allowed you to make threefold statements *simultaneously*, the kind of allegory Blake writes and Frye clarifies is like Bach. (Stingle 33)[4]

Reaney's emblems are prime examples of his making multi-levelled meanings as they present texts and pictures in action side by side.

The following exploration of James Reaney's work is organized on the basis of the emblems that he published as 'Two Chapters from an Emblem Book'. One at a time, each emblem will be used as a magnetic pole, while the opposite pole will consist of one or more of Reaney's other works. This procedure, derived from *Alphabet's* method, sets up a series of illuminating patterns — galaxies, even — in the lines of magnetic force between the poles.

---

1. See also my *University of Toronto Quarterly* article.
2. The images do recur, though, for instance in 'The Yellow-Bellied Sapsucker'. *Poems* 116.
3. Richard Stingle's article and Atwood's review are particularly illuminating with regard to Reaney's Congregationalist/Protestant formation.
4. Stingle is quoting from Reaney's 'The Identifier Effect' (28).

THE CASTLE

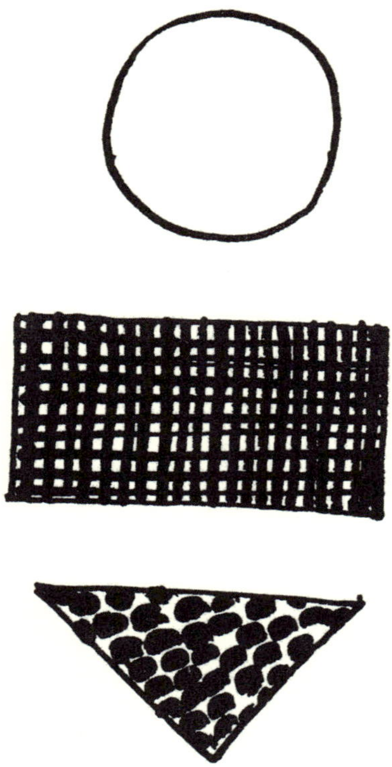

This is the ground plan
For a castle called Man

The Castle

What is man, that thou shouldst magnify him?
— Job 7: 17

The first of the five emblems in Chapter One of the unfinished Emblem Book is entitled 'The Castle'.[1] The simplicity of the drawing and the text, along with the title's and text's apparent incompatibility with the drawing, might cause readers to pass superficially over this emblem. However, closer examination is warranted.

The similar themes of 'The Castle' and Reaney's performance poem *One-man Masque* magnetically draw the works together, and this force field creates significant patterns of meaning. The emblem and the masque are also clear examples of Reaney's transformative aesthetic, noted previously as part of his reaction to the limitations of lyrical self-expression. In the course of a 1996 interview, Reaney said that in writing poetry 'You don't challenge yourself very much when you just use your own personal experience, whereas the kind of muse that Yeats and Blake and Milton had is a genuine otherness that you have to tackle, you have to work at. It's not easy. Or it's just confessing things' (Campbell 'Flow' 14). Directly relating to *One-man Masque,* in the Preface he wrote for the 2003 edition, Reaney tells us that in the fall of 1958, when his friend John Beckwith had asked him 'to fill the first part of an evening devoted to the première of *Night Blooming Cereus,* his first opera', Reaney was still intent on moving away from the lyric mode. He says that

> In the poetry readings I had been hearing at the time, Dylan Thomas, Edith Sitwell, and Allen Ginsberg (for example), what held them together was their authors' personalities. What I wanted to do was take a theme — Life and Death — what William Butler Yeats' epitaph expresses with: 'Cast a cold eye/On life, on death/ Horseman, pass by!' (i)

This leap from 'personalities' to 'a theme' is the same as that to be taken by Reaney's journal *Alphabet,* which he was about to launch, in 1960. As a theme, Yeats's epitaph (and no doubt also the volumes of Yeats's writings that Reaney had recently studied for his doctoral thesis) gave him further realization of a profound transformative pattern and source of metaphors fundamental to his own artistic vision:

> Until I'd read him I had never contemplated an alternative to the merry Protestant belief that we may ride by Life, but when we die, that's it — either Hell or Eternity and Stop!
>
> Yeats had ideas of Death as being a state we also passed through, possibly to Eternity, if we'd been worthy of it, or else we could sail on to reincarnation and have a try at Life again. (i)

Either way, death is not the end, but rather it is a stage on the human journey, a transformation. *One-man Masque* literally and emblematically enacts this journey, whisking the audience along with it. Read carefully, 'The Castle' also represents this theme. Like *One-man Masque,* the emblem requires substantial active interpretation by those who read it.

In a 1965 article in *Canadian Art* magazine, 'Search for an Undiscovered Alphabet', Reaney addresses the topic of diagrams as fundamental structural principles in a wide range of art and literature: 'Quite naturally, I suppose, the worlds of heraldry, insignia, typography, labels, advertisements and poetry come together in their search for an effective image. The search for the effective quite often leads to hieroglyph, pictograph, ideogram and diagram' (38). (A similar, more exclusively verbal search led Frye to postulate in *Anatomy of Criticism* a 'grammar of literary archetypes' [135].[2]) What can we make of the image and words of Reaney's 'The Castle'?

J.E. Cirlot says in his authoritative *Dictionary of Symbols* that symbolically, the castle combines the meanings of the house — 'the repository of all wisdom, that is, tradition itself' — and of the walled city — 'a symbol of the transcendent soul and of the heavenly Jerusalem'. He also notes that 'the sudden appearance of a castle in the path of a wanderer is like the sudden awareness of a spiritual pattern' (38). Another detail of this symbolism which Cirlot observes is that both the house and the walled city are generally considered to be feminine (47, 146).[3] The feminine aspects of the castle as a symbol open a tension caused by incorporating the masculine — a castle's towers, Reaney's vertical arrangement of the shapes, and his word 'Man' — along with traditionally feminine characteristics in one image. This recognition of the coexistence of opposites is a crucial part of the alchemical process, and as Jung explains, is often epitomized by a male-female conjunction:

> The brother-sister pair stands allegorically for the whole conception of opposites. These have a wide range of variation: dry-moist, hot-cold, male-female, sun-moon, gold-silver, mercury-sulphur, round-square, water-fire, volatile-solid, physical-spiritual, and so on. (317–18)

'The Castle', with its simple, archetypal circle, rectangle and triangle, evokes several sets of opposites and their coming together.

As well as this general symbolism, Reaney probably also had in mind a consistent and more specific meaning for the illustration component of 'The Castle', as his comments in the *Canadian Art* essay reveal. Recalling his thesis work, he writes:

> Yeats and Spenser present their readers with a series of diagrams, in which the circle represents a final reality. In Spenser's *Legend of Temperance*, Guyon and Arthur come to a castle which is partly triangular, partly circular with a quadrangle for its base. This is the Castle of Alma and it represents Man; the circular part of the castle stands for the intellectual soul and is spoken of as 'Immortall, perfect and masculine'; it represents a piece of Paradise within us: 'And likest is unto that heavenly towre, / That God hath built for his own blessed bowre.' (39)

Reaney might also have noted that the stanza from Canto 9, Book 2 of *The Faerie Queene*, in which the Castle of Alma is described diagrammatically, explicitly designates the castle's structure, 'a worke divine', as incorporating both the masculine circle, and also the feminine triangle. Spenser terms the triangle 'imperfect', meaning that the triangle represents change and movement, not finished perfection. Along with this reference, in the *Canadian Art* essay Reaney gives a sketch very much

'Prisoners in the Underworld.' *('Quis habitabit ex vobis cū ardorib? Sĕpitermus. Is. 33.')* From Sebastián Izquierdo's 1678 book, *Praxis exercitiorum spiritalium* (72). Rpt. In Jung 286.

like his emblem 'The Castle'. The sketch is entitled 'Spenser's Castle of Alma — a ground plan'. The rectangle and triangle in this drawing are simple outlines, whereas those shapes in 'The Castle' are more fully developed.

The cross-hatched rectangle in 'The Castle' recalls the Man in the Iron Cage from Bunyan, and other images of incarceration/death, such as 'Prisoners in the underworld'. Cirlot says that 'Of all geometric forms, the most rational, the most secure and regular' is the rectangle (260). The grid of horizontal and vertical lines which fills the rectangle, the centre of the Castle emblem, introduces the association of death with the cross: 'Placed in the mystic Centre of the cosmos, it becomes the bridge or ladder by means of which the soul may reach God' (Cirlot 65). Little ladders, which appear by combining the rectangle's multiple crosses, impart a further sense of an incomplete process, the realization that death is a necessary stage on the way to transformation.

Below the cross-hatched rectangle in Reaney's emblem is an inverted triangle filled with small semi-circular shapes. In the normal, apex-up position, the triangle 'symbolizes fire and the aspiration of all things towards the higher unity' (Cirlot 332); inverted, as in 'The Castle', the triangle stands for the opposites of fire and unity: water, as Reaney notes in 'Search for an Undiscovered Alphabet' (41), and division into multiplicity. Water is the state of matter both before it takes on form and after it dissolves. For this reason, according to Cirlot, the alchemists

> gave the name of 'water' to quicksilver in its first stage of transmutation and, by analogy, also to the 'fluid body' of man. This 'fluid body' is interpreted by modern psychology as a symbol of the unconscious, that is, of the non-formal, dynamic, motivating, female side of the personality. (345)

The inverted triangle of the unconscious may be seen as a complement to the rationality represented by the upwardly directed cross-hatching in the rectangle, and as a balance to the opposite, the 'masculine' circle.

An interpretation of the emblem as a whole — title, shapes and couplet — could be that symbolically it embodies the possibility for unity (the circle), and the striving through death for unity, both consciously (the rectangle with ladders), and unconsciously (the inverted triangle).

This interpretation would be directly in line not only with Spenser's Castle of Alma, a stage on a quest, but also with Jung's theory of human development as a process of individuation, the harmonizing of the conscious and unconscious aspects of the self. Jung writes,

> The symbols of the process of individuation that appear in dreams are images of an archetypal nature which depict the centralizing process or the production of a new centre of personality.... I call this centre the 'self', which should be understood as the totality of the psyche. The self is not only the centre but also the whole circumference which embraces both conscious and unconscious; it is the centre of this totality, just as the ego is the centre of the conscious mind. (41)

Reaney's emblem, it seems clear, can be understood as a symbolic recasting of the individuation process, complete with the active tensions which this process involves.

The words of the emblem suggest futurity — we are looking at 'the ground plan/For a castle called Man', not 'the ground plan/*Of* a castle called Man', which latter would imply that the castle has already been built. So, again comparably to Spenser's Castle of Alma, where Sir Guyon learns about Temperance as a virtue to be adopted as a foundation for living, Reaney's emblem suggests possibility and preparation, rather than achievement.

The relationship of the textual aspects to the illustration, similarly to this relationship in traditional emblems, is largely explanatory; the text aids the reader in comprehending the meanings of the symbolic images, primarily through offering starting-points for interpretation. The words indicate how we might decode the picture. As a 'ground plan', the illustration — as well as suggesting a future orientation — must be read as implying another dimension, just as topographical maps represent hills and valleys, and as blueprints imply three-dimensional buildings. In the case of the emblem, the further dimension is not so much spatial as symbolic.

Two other ideas from Jung's *Psychology and Alchemy* are helpful in explaining Reaney's impetus for creating such an emblem. As with Jung's distinguishing the personal unconscious from the collective unconscious, these explanations are individual *and* social. On the individual level, the following statement from *Psychology and Alchemy* might have caught the young emblem-maker Reaney's eye:

> Natural man is not a 'self' — he is the mass and the particle in the mass, collective to such a degree that he is not even sure of his own ego. That is why since time immemorial he has needed the transformation mysteries to turn him into something, and to rescue him from the animal collective psyche, which is nothing but a hodgepodge. (78)

This transformation process is not simply individualistic, then, but also works on the social plane, always a concern of Reaney's, expressed in his understanding of the Bible. Jung explains this dynamic:

> In an outward form of religion where all the emphasis is on the outward figure (hence where we are dealing with a more or less complete projection), the archetype is identical with externalized ideas but remains unconscious as a psychic factor. When an unconscious content is replaced by a projected image to that extent, it is cut off from all participation in and influence on the conscious mind.... It may easily happen, therefore, that a Christian who believes in all the sacred figures is still undeveloped and unchanged in his inmost soul because he has 'all God outside' and does not experience Him in the soul. His deciding motives, his ruling interests and impulses, do not spring from the sphere of Christianity, but from the unconscious and undeveloped psyche, which is as pagan and archaic as ever. Not the individual alone but the sum total of individual lives in a people proves the truth of this contention. The great events of our world as planned and executed by man do not breathe the spirit of Christianity, but rather of unadorned paganism....
>
> With the methods employed hitherto we have not succeeded in Christianizing the soul to the point where even the most elementary demands of Christian ethics can exert any decisive influence on the main concerns of the Christian European. Christianity must indeed begin again from the very beginning if it is to meet its

> high educative task. So long as religion is only faith and outward form, and the religious function is not experienced in our own souls, nothing of any importance has happened. It has yet to be understood that the *mysterium magnum* is not only an actuality but is first and foremost rooted in the human psyche. (11–12)

As was Jung, so was Reaney: a Protestant Christian. And so also was his most influential professor, Northrop Frye. Jung provided both Frye and Reaney not only with a sense of urgency about their work as teachers, but also with a model for connecting their contemporary societies and themselves with literature. Jung argues that

> Myth is the primordial language natural to these psychic processes, and no intellectual formulation comes anywhere near the richness and expressiveness of mythical imagery. Such processes deal with the primordial images, and these are best and most succinctly reproduced by figurative speech. (25)

To this statement, it would be reasonable to add, 'and symbolic pictures too' — of the sort Reaney created for his emblems. The alchemists' myths, elaborated by Jung as stories of psychic development, are fundamental to both Reaney's and Frye's work.

Perhaps the most conspicuous of the affinities that magnetically attract 'The Castle' and *One-man Masque* is that the word 'man' features prominently both in the emblem's rhyme and in the masque's title, signalling their themes. Both are hybrid forms: the emblem with its use of text and images; the masque with its use of a stage set with props, spoken language, physical actions, songs and dance. Also on a formal level, both 'The Castle' and *One-man Masque* are rooted in Renaissance models that Reaney thoroughly modernizes to dramatize the transformative processes that 'man' experiences. Reaney's 'Castle' emblem and *One-man Masque* present images of human life that emphasize the existence of contraries and the necessity of incorporating them into a unity. Masques, in fact, were often called 'emblems' during the Renaissance. With their hybrid natures, both types of artwork, the emblem and the masque, are well-suited to presenting Reaney's vision of all things occurring at once.

Emblems put words and visual images into play simultaneously to generate meanings. How does *One-man Masque* resemble this strategy?

There is a substantial body of literature on the subject of masques, so for the purposes of this exploration, I will only highlight some features of this European form of entertainment that are especially relevant to Reaney's work. In England, the masque flourished in the sixteenth and early seventeenth centuries, in the royal courts of Henry VIII, Elizabeth I, James I, and Charles I, as well as in the palaces of the nobility. The common people could have known directly about masques by seeing them as insertions in plays by Shakespeare, John Ford, Thomas Dekker and Thomas Nashe, for instance. Originally an Italian entertainment, English masques developed out of local folk customs involving disguises and mummery, and became a courtly form of celebration with elaborate, symbolical sets, costumes, torch-bearers, music and dances. Often the royal and aristocratic people in attendance, including women, unlike on public stages at the time, would themselves present the masques. Particularly during the reign of Henry VIII, a masque would sometimes conclude with the presenters' dancing with the audience, a prime opportunity for intrigue, no doubt. At the masque's height of development in England, the architect Inigo Jones (1573–1652) was the master scene maker; composers of music for masques included Thomas Campion, William Byrd, John Dowland, Alfonso Ferrabosco the Younger, and Giles Farnaby; the words for masques were written by Edmund Spenser — who also describes a masque of the Seven Deadly Sins in *The Faerie Queene* (Book I, Canto 4) — Philip Sidney, Francis Beaumont, Samuel Daniel, Ben Jonson and numerous others. A constant tension in the composition of masques was that between the spectacle, including the set, the costumes, the music and dancing, and the verbal.[4] This tension culminated in the breakup of Inigo Jones and Ben Jonson's collaboration. For students of English literature such as Reaney, the masque is studied largely because of Shakespeare's having composed brief masque-like plays-within-plays for several of his dramas: among them, *The Tempest, Love's Labour's Lost* and *A Midsummer Night's Dream*. When Jonson and others developed and wrote three-part masques divided into the anti-masque, the masque and the revel, Shakespeare's company, the Lord Chamberlain's Men, often performed the non-aristocratic anti-masques.

The subject matter of masques usually involved creating a flattering portrait of the monarch by casting her or him as a transcendent heroic figure from Classical or British mythology — perhaps Apollo or King Arthur, or for Elizabeth, Diana, Vesta, or the Queen of Faerie. The intent of this theme was not simply to please her or him and thereby gain royal favours, but it was educational too: as a paragon of Christian virtue, the monarch set an example for subjects to emulate. Also educational, especially with Jonson's masques, was the writers' vast erudition, displayed in the service of elaborating allegorical stories and exemplary characters.

By naming his performance poem *'One-man Masque'*, Reaney invokes the history, and more importantly, the conventions of the English masque form. This approach to a Renaissance genre is the same as his choosing to create emblems; and because of the erudition involved, it has led to Reaney's having been criticized for being too academic and thus not popular. However, there is an overriding argument. Without the audience's knowing much if anything about the pre-existent forms, nevertheless the weight of the forms' traditions contributes to the works' effects. In an extension of the audience's use of wit, they might be moved to learn more about the magnetic field of relationships generated between the antique forms and Reaney's adaptations of them. Conversely, but also involving audience participation, even without consciously knowing about the forms, people can be profoundly affected. Without knowing music history and theory, we can be moved emotionally by a song. Branwell, a character in Reaney's *A Suit of Nettles* nicely expresses this capacity:

> The meaning's felt often before it's seen;
> My heart knows what my rusted mind does not. (30)

Comparably, in all Roman Catholic church services until the mid-1960s, Latin was the language used, although the vast majority of the worshippers did not understand it. Nevertheless, even in the absence of linguistic comprehension, sacred ceremonies such as baptism, communion and marriage accomplished profoundly meaningful real-world results.

The script for *One-man Masque* begins with a precise description of the 'Scene', the stage setting for the masque. For what the set lacks in Renaissance lavishness, it amply compensates with symbolic intensity. Immediately, we are confronted with a circle, the centre and circumference that constitute the self, noted already in connection with 'The Castle'. The circular action of the masque, guided by the set and props, as Ross Woodman pointed out (23), is reminiscent of the life circles movement in Blake's poem 'The Mental Traveller'. Here is the entire 'Scene' description:

> *The curtain rises to reveal a collection of objects arranged in a circle.*
>
> *Starting on the left we have a cradle, a baby carriage, a child's chair, a big chair, a table, a bed, a rocking chair and a coffin. This line of objects fills the extreme front of the stage.*
>
> *Now, starting near the coffin and circling back towards the cradle again we have another line of objects: a hall tree, a rain barrel, a section of stairs, a dresser with a mirror, a tree branch, a ladder, a spinning-wheel, and a cardboard box.*
>
> *The cardboard box loops us back to the cradle again.*
>
> *In the centre of the circle, as an onstage audience, there should be two mannequins sitting on false chairs, a man and a woman.*
>
> *Enter a live man with a closed umbrella.* (38)

The 'live man' proceeds to introduce these objects to the 'ladies and gentlemen' of the audience, saying that the stage front objects make up the 'gentleman of life', while the objects to the rear compose 'Lady Death'. Including the mannequins as an onstage audience also emphasizes the point that this masque is about all of us, and that we all need reviving.

One-man Masque, like the 'Castle' emblem, poses a visual and verbal conundrum. With the emblem, the question is, in what ways is the picture, called a 'castle', related to the verse, a metaphor stating that 'This is the ground plan/For a castle called Man.' We have, at least partially, unravelled that knot. With the masque, before the 'Man' introduces the objects, he states the work's conundrum:

> Ladies and gentlemen, life is extremely difficult to define. Ladies and gentlemen are extremely difficult to define. There is the life called life which is mysterious. There is the life called death which is unknown. You might say that life was a gentleman and death was a lady. (38)

These words could equally serve as a description of 'The Castle'. And what, we wonder, do the words have to do with all of the objects on stage? Both works in their unique ways announce that wit is required in order to understand what we are beholding.

It is not too much of a stretch to say that *One-man Masque's* opening is an emblem, consisting as it does both of visual elements — the objects shaping a circle on the stage, the man with his umbrella, the mannequin audience — and of verbal elements — the man's speech. *One-man Masque* differs from 'The Castle' in that the word component is not written, but instead delivered orally. Because of the different formal possibilities, the masque develops its meanings differently from the way that the emblem does, even though the works' themes are close. While the emblem's reader and the masque's audience experience the artworks with different senses, there are remarkable correspondences both thematically and on the level of process, in how Reaney's masque and emblem work.

• Active participation is required of the masque's audience and the emblem's viewer; they all need to exercise their wit. The mannequins on stage drive home this requirement in *One-man Masque.* The audience is integral to the performance.
• Both the emblem and the masque appeal to individual readers and to groups. While the person who contemplates an emblem might be alone in a room, as might a reader of the script of *One-man Masque,* both people come to realize that they are inextricably connected with an enormous cultural and historical matrix. If they do not recognize this condition at first, surely they will once they use their wit. As his career progressed, Reaney increasingly involved himself in constructing dramas, partly because the cultural connections on which his works are based come to life palpably in performance.
• These cultural connections are particularly evident in 'The Castle' and *One-man Masque* as symbolism. The emblem's illustration and written words, and the masque's arrangement of props and spoken words both require symbolic thought and draw on the same source domains for their symbolic power. As mentioned, some of these domains — and the range is wider yet, as we shall see, — are Spenser's and Yeats's poetry, and Jung's psychoanalytic writings.
• The emblem and the masque both exhibit Reaney's play-box-style, all-

at-once visual and verbal moment. In *One-man Masque* the visual aspect, the circular set, creates all-at-once unity. Reaney once described the *One-man Masque* set as 'a series of tableaux and spectacles, or stage images' ('Babble' 42).

• Simultaneously, though, both operate in time too: meaning develops as the emblem reader employs wit, just as meaning develops for the wit-employing audience as the masque is played out. In neither case is the dawn of meaning instantaneous, but rather, takes time.

After the 'live man' in *One-man Masque* names the objects arranged in a circle onstage he demonstrates, in a way that is easy for the audience to grasp, how symbolism works. The stage directions say, *'He picks up the child's chair, puts it on his knee and talks to it'* (39). By mentally taking the small step of linking the chair with its probable user, a child, the man and the audience are able to — and do — comprehend the small chair symbolically, as standing for the child. This sequence is *One-man Masque's* way of announcing how it is to be understood. It is now simple for all to see the props laid out in a circle on the stage as phases 'of life, of life and death' (38).

The living man then says to the child/chair:

> And so you want to live? How does one breathe? At first it was not easy. Long ago our ancestors did not breathe. They simply were. They wered. But they dreamed of breathing. One day someone discovered that lungs were filled with air. Everyone breathed out and there was lots of air for everybody so that everybody could breathe. (39)

The import of this little myth is multi-dimensional. It reverses the so-called normal, scientific ideas that breathing is necessary for life to exist, and that no one decides to breathe, because they are already breathing involuntarily. But the 'living man' is blurring boundaries, in particular those between life and death. He is also claiming for people a state of pure being that precedes the overlaying of concepts and conditions that we impose on our selves. Most of us perceive these mental laws of logic and causality as prerequisite, unalterable and final; but the living man's story, of a human dream's becoming the way it might be, at least questions what Blake in his poem 'London' called 'mind-forg'd manacles' and opens the possibility for our imaginations to work. The living man's telling a story, making up a myth, is his revelation of his imagination at work — or should the word be 'play'? (It is noteworthy in this chapter about 'The Castle' that Blake's 'London' also refers to 'Palace walls' in an image of human self-inflicted suffering.)

Following this movement, the living man applies the same imaginative technique to space and time; with figurative speech, in Jung's terms, he creates a primordial myth (see page 42). In response to the question 'How does one live?' the man tells the chair / child that

> you mix up time and space. Space? Space is when you reach into your head for the red ball you see there and it isn't there! It's out there — somewhere! Put on your eyes — you're blind without them.
>
> Time? Time is when you see a thing out there and later on you don't see it out there. But you can only see it in here. So there's been a thing called time come along. (39)

So, as with assumptions about breathing, space and time are revealed not as natural or inevitable, but rather as human constructs to explain developments in human beings.

The masque next changes to a dance along the semi-circle of death objects. The living man tells the child / chair that

> Living is as easy as — opening an umbrella!
>
> Stage direction: '*He opens the umbrella and skips around the circle of objects* ... (39).

This dramatic transition is emblematized by the sudden metamorphosis of the umbrella's shape from thin straight cylinder to big round circle. The man's sitting and talking with the chair changes to the children's activity of skipping merrily, umbrella raised. He revisits the Death objects, again ending with the small chair, which he raises 'triumphantly'. This time, the small chair has become a baby; we are in a world where time itself does not obey clocks, but travels in circles of the imagination's devising.

The living man then speaks the 'Baby' poem, which begins by presenting the baby in the uterus building himself:

> I made the tooth
> I invented the eye
> I played out hair on a comb harp
> I thought up the sigh. (40)

This busy self-identifying baby is a hero, conquering many hazards and coming to terms with two mysterious gifts: the 'vorpal phallus/Filled with jostling army', and the 'magic tongue/Stuffed with names and numbers' (41). 'Vorpal', wonderfully appropriate in this context, is a word made up by Lewis Carroll in *Through the Looking-glass* to describe a blade, meaning it is keen and deadly. At once, the phallus is creator and destroyer. The tongue, though, is 'The waker from fallen slumbers'. As the container and vehicle of language, the tongue holds the possibility of people's becoming conscious of themselves through words, as the real agents of their own destinies.

However, such promise is not fulfilled for the *in utero* baby; birth is a setback, occurring just when he had almost accomplished illumination:

> My mother opened her grave,
> I sprang out a giant
> Into another cave
> Where I was a seed again.
>
> Hapless and wriggly small
> As in my father's groin:
> My Shakespeare's tongue a wawl
> And impotent my loin. (41)

Another round of development begins, a search for light while fending off the enslaving and blinding chains of convention. The 'Baby' poem ends with the same verse as its first verse: 'Small babe, tell me/As you sit in your mother's cave/What do you build there,/Little baby mine?' (42). The cave for the baby now is not the uterus, but the world in which we all see darkly.

One-man Masque proceeds circularly to explore in detail features of this shadowy life and death: childhood, adolescence, marriage, child-rearing, old age, 'Death's World', and Doomsday. In the Doomsday section of the masque the living man, now called the speaker, *'stands in front of the dresser and yells through the megaphone'*. The dresser contains the 'old flesh dresses' needed for the 'resurrection parties and balls' (54). It also has a mirror, indicating that even though we might feel that it doesn't, doomsday, or the apocalypse, does include the one in the mirror too. With doomsday in mind, readers of Reaney's 'Castle' emblem and of *One-man Masque* sense a powerful magnetic field taking shape. The living man becomes a dwarf; he shrinks, an unmistakeable sign that another round of childhood is about to commence. The dwarf tells the story of his life, starting with

> Six inches of my six foot Pa
> Compressed my height to these three feet.
> On Sabbath day he sold me to
> The castle of the starry street.
>
> There I sleep in a cradle and amuse
> The castle with my minority.
> No, I am not someone far away.
> Reach out and touch me. (55–6)

The 'castle of the starry street', like Spenser's Castle of Alma in *The Faerie Queene* and Reaney's 'Castle' emblem, provides opportunities for learning life lessons. The dwarf in *One-man Masque,* though, is a teacher, one who inverts appearances. He is not 'far away'; rather, he is a small man, the embodiment of contraries, but lacking full humanity nevertheless. Instead of constructively transforming the castle, the dwarf mock-apocalyptically destroys it:

> The castle's empty, wonder none —
> I bade them rebuild inside out.
> Their fire flew up into the sun,
> Their cistern rolled into a moon. (57)

At this point, the dwarf is approaching the nadir of his life-in-death trajectory, 'holed up here among the ruins/The compressed cause of everything' (57). The ruins of the symbolic castle indicate that the dwarf's journey to enlightenment has been stalled by his self-absorption. He is a Job figure now, in despair. Here are some lines spoken by Job that reverberate with the dwarf's predicament:

> When I say, My bed shall comfort me, my couch shall ease my complaints,
> Then thou scarest me with dreams, and terrifiest me through visions:
> So that my soul chooseth strangling, and death rather than my life.
> I loathe it; I would not live alway: let me alone; for my days are vanity.
> What is man, that thou shouldest magnify him? and that thou shouldest set thine heart upon him? (Job 7: 13–17)

Reaney's 'Castle' emblem offers an answer to Job's question, 'What is man?': namely, a work in progress. In terms of the imagery of 'The Castle', the dwarf is caught behind the crossed bars of the rectangle. In addition to being a sign of self-absorption, when the dwarf says that he is the 'compressed cause of everything', the statement is also true. Saying it thus leads to the dwarf's immediately admitting that 'The only thing I know to do/Is crawl into this manger.' This knowledge and the crawling action echo Job's infantile retreat to his bed for comfort. However, the manger suggests to the dwarf Christ's birthplace, and he proceeds to utter a debasing, animalistic parody of the biblical nativity event:

> I'll prop the dead queen's body up,
> Perhaps 'twill fool a stranger.
>
> Come here shepherds. Here's the way.
> Bah bah bah for an incarnation.
> This way aristocratic intelligence.
> Meow meow for a new sensation!

To the curious observant baby
The humble and the royal bow.
Hush-a-bye my baby do, for see —
The spider on your mother's brow. (57)

This last line is a verbal emblem. In Jungian terms, the dead queen/mother indicates that the speaker, who at this point is not the dwarf, has come to terms with the feminine side of his self, and is ready to move on by a rebirth to the actualization of his whole self. The spider reinforces this interpretation since through its attributes of creation (its web) and destruction (the prey caught in the web) the spider symbolizes the alternating forces that generate our world. 'For this reason,' Cirlot observes, 'the symbolism of the spider goes deep, signifying, as it does, that 'continuous sacrifice' which is the means of man's continual transmutation throughout the course of his life' (290).

The final phase of *One-man Masque* is called 'The Lost Child'. In part, this lost child is the epiphany that just occurred in the malign manger scene, a false messiah trying to 'fool a stranger' into believing that it was a positive, spiritual birth, when instead it was a lost opportunity to grow and to embrace the future. This lost chance is also represented by the baby's diabolically being told to 'hush-a-bye' rather than to act upon the truth that could be realized by means of the spider on the mother's brow emblem. Being quiet, without language, the baby becomes, sadly, the lost child. Perhaps this silencing of the baby is why, unlike the 'Dwarf' section of *One-man Masque,* 'The Lost Child' is not narrated by the title character. The speaker is the 'living man', but caught in Death's World again.

This world is portrayed as wintertime, and although the child is lost, the speaker detects his presence in everything he notices. Here are the first four stanzas of the 'Lost Child' poem:

Long have I looked for my lost child
I hear him shake his rattle
Slyly in the winter wind
In the ditch that's filled with snow

He pinched and shrieked and ran away

At the edge of the November forest.
The hungry old burdock stood
By the dry dead ferns.

Hear him thud that ball!
The acorns fall by the fence.
See him loll in the St. Lucy sun,
The abandoned sheaf in the wire.

Oh life in Death! My bonny nursling
Merry drummer in the nut brown coffin,
With vast wings outspread I float
Looking and looking over the empty sea. (58)

Rattles are traditionally made from gourds, the hardened seed pods of squash-like plants. The lost child rattling seeds in the snowy ditch suggests the possibility of new life arising from below ground. The death images of the leafless forest, the burdock and the ferns imply their rebirth in spring, as the acorns also suggest the possibility for new life. St. Lucy's Day, December 13th, is still celebrated by many Scandinavians as the winter solstice, that is, the turning of the old year into the new. John Donne's poem 'A Nocturnal Upon S. Lucy's Day, Being the Shortest Day', connects St. Lucy's Day to the poet's state of despair.[5] Lolling in that day's sun, the lost child appears as an 'abandoned sheaf in the wire'. The sheaf in the wire symbolizes being bound to the material plane of existence, the inability to move to the spiritual level; conversely, the sheaf stands for 'unification, integration and strength' (Cirlot 280). So even in the winter setting, there is promise of renewal, and the lost child is sensed as a 'bonny nursling/Merry drummer in the nut brown coffin'.

One-man Masque's stage directions indicate that the 'vast wings outspread' derive from John Milton's famous invocation at the opening of *Paradise Lost*, as does the phrase 'empty sea':

And chiefly thou, O Spirit, that dost prefer
Before all temples the upright heart and pure,
Instruct me for thou know'st; Thou from the first
Wast present and with mighty wings outspread

> Dove-like sat'st brooding on the vast abyss,
> And mad'st it pregnant: what in me is dark,
> Illumine; what is low, raise and support;
> That to the highth of this great argument
> I may assert Eternal Providence,
> And justify the ways of God to men. (Book I: 17–26)

Reaney's alluding to these particular lines from the beginning of *Paradise Lost* at this moment, nearly at the close of *One-man Masque,* is telling. The passage from *Paradise Lost* presents a poet praying for help with the daunting task of composing a hugely ambitious epic. In *One-man Masque* the silenced baby who is now the lost child has at least begun to make rattling and drumming sounds, showing that there is promise for fuller communication. As compared to *Paradise Lost,* in *One-man Masque* it is not the dove of God's spirit 'brooding on the vast abyss'; it is the living man, 'Looking and looking over the empty sea'. There is indeed a parallel in the situations, but *One-man Masque* is distinctly indicating, again, that the 'waker from fallen slumbers' (41), the agent of a person's attaining creative power — 'recreative power' would be a better way to put it — is in the person's own tongue, language.

'The Lost Child' segment ends hopefully, as the man 'rescues' his lost child, imagined to be in the 'cradle by the coffin'. He says the following lines '*kneeling like a shepherd at Christ's Cradle*':

> And there! In the — on the rolling death
> Rattling a dried out gourd
> Floated the mysterious cradle
> Filled with a source.
>
> I push the shore and kingdom to you,
> O winter walk with seed pod ditch:
> I touch them to the floating child
> And lo! Cities and gardens, shepherds and smiths. (58)

To emphasize the masque's intention to be a process that involves us all, the man's words are directed to the audience, not to the child. This summarizing speech reprises images from earlier in *One-man Masque:* the

Miltonic 'vast abyss' ('rolling death'), the stirrings of communication ('Rattling'), the ruined castle's 'cistern' now successfully transformed into a 'source'.

The man then offers to the audience 'the shore', a place to stand after the disorientation of the sea-like abyss of 'rolling death'. The word 'kingdom' evokes for us the 'Castle' emblem, a connection that intensifies our understanding that this gift is the possibility to enter the kingdom of our true humanity, 'a ground plan / For a castle called Man'. With the words 'O winter walk with seed pod ditch', he names us, the audience, by the figurative situation in which we find ourselves: the season of death, yet with signs of new life in even the most ordinary places. With his ceremonial gesture of 'touch[ing] them to the floating child', a vision of renewed human life appears, all products and kinds of human labour: 'Cities and gardens, shepherds and smiths' (58).

The finale of *One-man Masque* combines actions as well as words. The man returns the cradle to its original spot, away from the coffin. Then '*he is handed a tray of lighted candles*', and, bringing the performance full circle, he repeats the words he said at the start of the masque: 'Ladies and gentlemen, Life and Death are indeed difficult to define' (59). An effect of this repetition is to bracket the performance that we have just witnessed, to unify it as a circle, and transform the masque from a linear sequence into a moment of realization. Now '*The speaker lifts the tray of lighted candles up and puts them on his head*' (59). No one who celebrates the triumph of St. Lucy, the patron saint of blind people and of writers, would miss the symbolism involved in this emblematic act. 'Lucy' — the original Sicilian saint's name was 'Lucia' — derives from the Latin word for 'light', '*lux/lucis*'. To commemorate Lucia's God-given imperviousness to torture by burning, and also to acknowledge her bringing of light on the darkest night of the year, a woman masquerades as St. Lucy, and wears a wreath of lighted candles on her head. In *One-man Masque* the living man's action embodies the masque's theme of finding light in a dark time and place. The action is also ceremonial, recalling the point made earlier, that for the audience, even if they do not fully consciously grasp what is happening, the ritual action still produces its magical effects. *One-man Masque* provides an emblem of this insight as well. While the man wears his candle hat, the final stage directions say, '*The two mannequins float up and disappear*' (59). The onstage audience quit the scene, leaving the audience role to the people present. In the Preface to the 2003 edition of *One-man Masque,* Reaney recounts the audience's enthusiasm at the end of a performance of the masque by Jeff Culbert at London's Grand Theatre about a year before:

> There were even screams for the last image of *One-man Masque* when Jeff took a tray of five candles, lit them, and balanced the tray on his head! It was electrifying. (iii)

The 'image' is an emblem, as is the masque as a whole: 'a ground plan / For a castle called Man'. Reaney, who was seventy-six at the time, writes that the production created 'startling effects': 'Seeing this Ausable Theatre production made me feel young again' (iv). No doubt he wasn't surprised.

---

1. The 'Castle' and the following Reaney emblems are reproduced with the permission of Reaney (telephone conversation, 26 April 2002) and subsequently of James Stewart Reaney and Susan Wallace. The title in Warkentin's edition, 'Two Chapters from an Emblem Book, 1969–70', may be slightly misleading. These are all the chapters and emblems that he published. Two unpublished emblems were displayed at the 2008 McMichael exhibition (L2007.7.55).
2. John Ayre's article thoroughly explores this topic with relation to Frye.
3. This feminine aspect might seem to be at odds with the last word of Reaney's text, 'Man'; however, 'Man' here and elsewhere in Reaney's work was not meant to be as gender-specific as it is nowadays. The practice of using 'Man' to indicate both female and male human beings was just beginning to end in the 1960s, with the influence of second-wave feminism.
4. Peter Walls details this tension.
5. Clarence H. Miller goes into detail about the poem's relations with the Nocturns church service.

The Farm

'Cities and gardens, shepherds and smiths': to the living man's list of human productions and occupations at the close of *One-man Masque,* we could add 'farms', although 'shepherds' might convey much of what 'farms' stand for. In the pastoral tradition of literature, farms are ideal places, part way between the temptations and decadence of cities and the diverse dangers of 'Nature, red in tooth and claw', as Tennyson puts it. Following the classical models of Theocritus' *Bucolics* in Greek, and Virgil's *Eclogues* in Latin, English Renaissance poets set their pastoral eclogues on farms, with shepherds as characters. ('Eclogues', derived from Greek, means 'selections'.) As did the Roman poet Virgil, the English Renaissance poets typically had satiric intentions, and the shepherds' dialogues addressed existing social problems. Often the shepherds were recognizable contemporary figures masked in rustic costumes. Sir Edmund Spenser's *The Shepheardes Calender,* of 1579, is a series of twelve English eclogues, one devoted to each month of the year. Spenser scholar Reaney used the form and themes of *The Shepheardes Calender* for his 1958 volume titled *A Suit of Nettles,* a series of satirical selections which won that year's Governor General's Award for poetry. Instead of shepherds, though, *A Suit of Nettles* is populated with geese.

Germaine Warkentin's introduction to Reaney's *Poems* suggests the importance to him of his family farm:

> Born near Stratford in 1926, to a family evangelical in religion and of mixed Scottish, Irish and German origin, Reaney still retains at the centre of his poetic world the farm on which he was born.... Of all the images that his essentially symbolist poetic dwells on, the most recurrent are the farm terrain (seen both as a fruitful orchard and neglected garden) and the true and false parents that surround the 'lost children' of his poems and dramas. (ix)

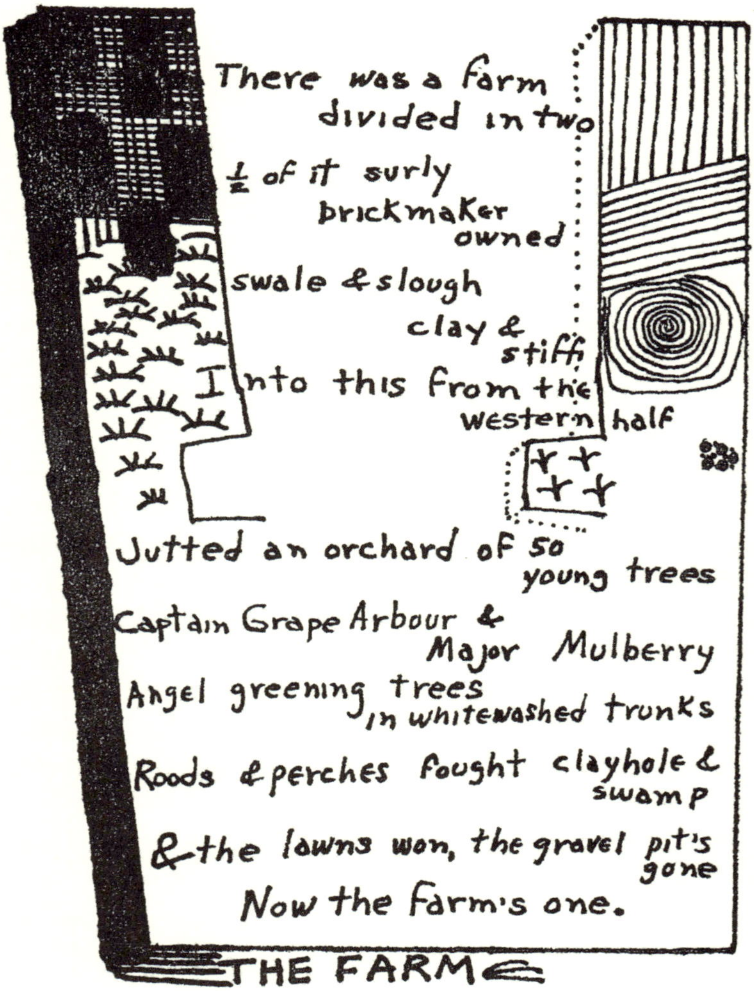
There was a farm
divided in two
½ of it surly
brickmaker
owned
swale & slough
clay &
stiff
Into this from the
western half
Jutted an orchard of 50
young trees
Captain Grape Arbour &
Major Mulberry
Angel greening trees
in whitewashed trunks
Roods & perches fought clayhole &
swamp
& the lawns won, the gravel pit's
gone
Now the farm's one.
THE FARM

Reaney's 'The Farm' emblem expresses both the farm's fruitful, giving aspects and its damaged, exploited side. The emblem's overall shape suggests a horseshoe magnet, the words between the branches being the magnetic field's lines.

Another farm that is important to Reaney and that is related to this emblem is the farm in *The Kálevála,* the Finnish 'national visionary poem'. He explains in 'Vision in Canada?' that *The Kálevála* 'is about the conflict between North Farm and South Farm with a central hero — a bard, a poet, older than his bride.' This conflict is 'a battle between the two forces of death (North Farm) and life (South Farm)' (937). His September poem, 'Mythos', in *Performance Poems* (88–93) similarly displaces *The Kálevála* to contrast Noresto (Northeastern Ontario) with Souwesto. The 'Farm' emblem is divided East/West, but the archetypal pattern of conflict is present in *The Kálevála,* 'Mythos' and the emblem.

The emblem is a distorted rectangle, wider at the top on account of the division of the cultivated from the quarried areas of the farm. Further, the map is drawn with South at the top (the orchard is jutting from the West), an inversion of the usual north-south orientation of maps, also suggesting that things are out of kilter. The dark 'clayhole and swamp' in this inverted projection are on the left of the map to indicate that they are on the sinister side. These features of the bisected farm are represented by a combination of black rectangles, possibly clay bricks, on a grid that recalls the death symbolism of the cross-hatched rectangle in 'The Castle'. As Northrop Frye explains in *Fearful Symmetry,* a brick represents for William Blake oppression because the Jews were forced to make bricks for the Pyramids during their captivity. The brick, Frye says, 'is a symbol of a mathematic form constructed out of the deadest part of the material world' (364). The circle fragments with three rays each seem to stand for the wasted land that barely supports life. In a section titled 'Roberts' Clayhole & Brickyard', from the sequence 'Little Lake District (Where I was Born)', Reaney writes that after yielding the materials for many of the Stratford community's buildings, 'Now, cedar stumps, snipe, rain-filled scow,/Water fills my communal source now' (*Souwesto Home* 25). The 'orchard' side of the farm contains parallel lines representing the furrows of ploughed, trapezoidal fields. Not being as regular as rectangles, having only one pair of parallel sides, these shapes reinforce the sense that the wholeness of the farm has been disrupted. Contrary to this negativity, however, are the spiral, a form that suggests evolution and growth, and four 'Angel greening trees', clear signals of imminent change for the better. Like thick, out-of-joint puzzle pieces, the halves of the farm in the picture plead to be brought together. As though in response, the words of the emblem do just that.

Paradoxically, given this healing movement, the predominant metaphor in the latter part of the emblem's verse is warfare. The '50 young trees' *jut* into the 'swale and slough / clay and stiff', a verb with violent connotations. When 'The Farm' mentions 'Captain Grape Arbour & Major Mulberry', these military personifications, which bring to mind Spenser and Bunyan's allegorical names, are still fruit-bearing plants. They are engaged in a just war, it seems, as they set out figuratively to humanize the quarry side of the farm.[1] It is important to note that the goal of this war is unity, not necessarily symmetry. During an interview published in the *Windsor Review,* Reaney offered Wanda Campbell his thoughts on why Ontario is a 'sacred place', and why this sacredness is sometimes difficult to appreciate:

> We have to deal with the fact that we had a cadastral survey that did everything at right angles, and you don't get a very interesting landscape when everything is chopped up into 90 degree angles. You have to fight that.... Our lane, for example, at home, our lane is not at right angles with anything. My theory about culture is that you have to have a crooked road, which is the road in front of our farm, because there were three families that were very interested in art there.... It was partly that they lived in an area where you couldn't quite get it all, you couldn't quite see it right down to the end, the way to get to the town. You can put two and two together. A couple of swamps helped. (18)

'Cadastral' is from a Greek term, 'κατα στικηον', meaning 'by the line'. Such a survey stands in direct contradiction to Blake's Proverb of Hell: 'Improve[m]ent makes strait roads, but the crooked roads without Improvement, are roads of Genius' (*Marriage,* Plate 10). Reaney's 'theory', an exposition in personal terms of Blake's Proverb, contributes to our understanding of the grid and black rectangles of the 'surly brickmaker' side of his emblem 'The Farm'. More generally too, the theory that a developing culture is aided by being 'in an area where you couldn't quite get it all', can be helpful in understanding the role of such local details in Reaney's works.

Like 'The Farm', *A Suit of Nettles* exemplifies the often-noted feature of Reaney's work, that it is regional — 'Regional' with a capital 'R'. Reaney's Regionalism is much more than local colour, though, and it is much more than autobiography. Perhaps because some of his works were published during the 1950s, '60s, and '70s, decades when Canadian nationalism was being strenuously encouraged, the presence of Southwestern Ontario in Reaney's poems and plays has been regarded as promotional, an attempt to bring prominence to a neglected part of the world. Supporting this argument is the fact that in 1579, when Spenser published *The Shepheardes Calender*, England was at a similar turning point to Canada's in the 1950s, '60s and '70s, being at that time involved in a search for English, instead of pan-European, literary forms and content. Consider how much the following description of Spenser's position, from Ernest de Selincourt's introduction to the collection of Spenser's works that Reaney could well have read, might also apply to Reaney's situation in the Canada of the late 1950s:

> The spread of education, the influence of the learning and culture of the Renaissance, the habit of foreign travel, the awakening of a national consciousness, had all tended to create a public eagerly interested in literature, and especially in poetry.... Spenser realized the situation and set himself to fulfil the demand. And he was able to fulfil it because, though he was himself steeped in all that was accounted learning by his contemporaries, he turned for his vital inspiration to that fountain of native poetry which they for the most part ignored. (xiv–xv)

A view that emphasizes historical opportunism less than aesthetic concerns is that the local details are necessary compositional elements — necessary, that is, to creating a unity of local and universal. (As we saw with 'The Castle' and with *One-man Masque,* the local–universal opposition is not explicitly at play in all of Reaney's works, while different contraries might be.) An early critic of Reaney's work, Alvin Lee, puts the case bluntly and correctly:

> For all his interest in things Canadian, it is clear that the major impetus is the desire to induce others to escape the dreary actuality of the environment. (133)

'To see a world in a grain of sand', the opening line of William Blake's poem 'Auguries of Innocence', is apposite in this context. The gist is not that the 'world' is *superior* to the 'grain of sand', but that the infinitely large requires the quantifiably tiny. Similar to the polar opposites of a magnet, the 'world' and the 'grain of sand' generate a field of forces, patterns in common, as do the regional and the universal in Reaney's work. As in 'The Farm', sometimes these poles are in conflict, as the war metaphors indicate. How do such dynamic patterns of meaning work in *A Suit of Nettles*?

For epigraphs to *A Suit of Nettles,* Reaney uses a series of quotations referring to geese. He is alerting the reader to the poem's unconventional yet appropriate casting of geese as its main characters. These epigraphs are titled with alphabet letters from 'A' to 'N'. Two in particular, 'H' and 'I', draw the attention of readers attuned to Reaney's emblems:

> H
>
> *What a goose you are.* In the Egyptian hieroglyphics the emblem of a vain silly fellow is a goose.
>
> I
>
> The coat of arms of the Company of Musicians — viz., a swan, with expanded wings, within a double tressure [the gridiron], counter, flory, argent. Perverted into a goose striking the bars of a gridiron with its foot, and called 'The Swan and Harp', or 'Goose and Gridiron'.[2]

The 'H' quotation suggests emblematically that *A Suit of Nettles* will be concerned to some degree with folly; that is, it will be satirical. The 'I' quotation, a verbal representation of an emblem and how it was 'perverted', also indicates that satirical deflation of pretensions is a method of *A Suit of Nettles.* In locating the poem in a barnyard with geese for characters, Reaney is already demonstrating such deflation from the sophistication of Spenser's eclogues. At the same time, Reaney was probably aware that even though the swan as an emblem is associated with the

Greek god Apollo, swans are silent birds — mute until just before they die, so legend has it, when they utter their swan song. Geese, on the other hand, are highly vocal, communicative birds, and besides, their feathers were for centuries the writer's tool of choice. So on a practical level, geese are suitable to enact satire and at times to be its butt.

'The Swan and Harp':
The Arms of the Worshipful Company of Musicians, 1604.

Following these epigraphs, and just before the first eclogue, 'January', Reaney sets an 'Invocation to the Muse of Satire'. Satire is a mode of writing in a medley of styles, with the aim of ridiculing and correcting folly; it is ancient. However, a muse of satire is not included in the lists of Greek muses, who are the daughters of Memory. Reaney is far more interested in imagination than memory. His invented muse is urged by the poet, 'With Punch's stick (he holds it in his hand) / Beat fertility into a sterile land.' Punch is the English and Canadian descendant of the furiously critical puppet Pulcinella of the sixteenth-century Italian *commedia dell'arte* tradition. The poet's Invocation goes on to concoct a verbal emblem of the Muse of Satire, 'With hands of hawthorn branches in the winter, / And teeth of cold March rain that bite the soft snow', and so on, down to her 'feet with harrows, and with discs for shoes' (11). So the poet's muse, wielding Punch's stick, is characterized as having elements of chaotic irrationality and slapstick humour, as well as the physical means to revive the land. This renewal is not only on the level of vegetation, of course, and the twelve month-named eclogues to come specify areas of human life that are in need of the muse's corrective attention. The poet's wish for her effect is ultimately apocalyptic: 'May you make the sky red with doom and axey wrath,' he writes. As with the 'Farm' emblem, *A Suit of Nettles* includes in its prescription for improvement a strong dose of conflict.

The January eclogue is a discussion between the geese Branwell and Mopsus. Branwell, wearing a green suit of stinging nettle leaves to torture himself, is also in a state of emotional self-torture. He is melancholy because he is 'Crossed in love'; he doubts to the point of questioning the worth of life. Mopsus responds to Branwell's question whether 'all life should cease' by saying that it would cease if everyone stopped going along with the rhythms of nature by refusing sexual love or else becoming a hermit. Showing some start-of-the-year hope, Branwell wonders, 'But should we smother all creation outright?' Mopsus advises him to reject the contraries he has outlined, lustiness and asceticism, and instead, develop their Platonic friendship in 'ferny groves by calm canals / Where all is bland correct and rational'. He promises that they would become so oblivious to physicality that death would only seem to be 'a change in weather'. Branwell finds this prospect chilling and abhorrent; to display his vitality, in a way that suggests it is beyond his conscious control,

Branwell's language transmutes into a Gerard Manley Hopkins vein. To Mopsus he says, concluding the January eclogue,

> Your favourite land is better I agree —
> What a round concrete continent of snows!
> But too round and too continent for me
> For I want offspring summerson autumnman wintersage
> And tricklerain thawwind panetap upleaf windrage
> Plow and seed and hoe, green, sucklepig, yellowripe,
> sicklestraw and all such glamourie.

The magic of life that Branwell prefers to Mopsus's bloodlessly perfect world emerges from the transformed language itself. 'Too round', we recognize as emblem language indicating overly finished and static. The Hopkins poem that Branwell's speech particularly brings to mind is 'Pied Beauty', which also expresses, albeit in a religious idiom, the poet's revelling in the higgledy-piggledy aspects of life:

> Glory be to God for dappled things —
> For skies of couple-colour as a brinded cow;
> For rose-moles all in stipple upon trout that swim;
> Fresh-firecoal chestnut-falls; finches' wings;
> Landscape plotted and pieced — fold, fallow, and plough;
> And áll trades, their gear and tackle and trim.
>
> All things counter, original, spáre, strange;
> Whatever is fickle, frecklèd (who knows how?)
> With swíft, slów; sweet, sóur; adázzle, dím;
> He fathers-forth whose beauty is pást change:
> Práise hím.

'Pied Beauty', like 'The Farm', and like the January eclogue, encompasses contraries. None of the three works stifles the differences, but rather regards them as integral to being alive. Punch's stick in *A Suit of Nettles,* in fact, does not merely administer Three-Stooges-style slaps, but it stirs up profound disagreements, for instance, about how best to live one's life. Considering Punch's stick as a stimulant, it is possible to interpret

Branwell's wearing of such a prickly suit as a way for him to avoid letting his mood dip further than melancholy, and into indifference.

The February eclogue presents Branwell's 'reckless hope' of attaining Dorcas's affection in altogether different language, that of the Renaissance convention of courtly love poetry:

> My love I give to you a threefold thing,
> A jewsharp serenade, a song I've made
> And a sparkling pretty rose diamond ring.
> To haste your love to me by fate delayed.
> Zing zing zing zing, azeezing, azeezing,
> Azuggazing, azeezug-zug-azing.

The last two lines represent the sound of the jewsharp, I presume. Anyway, however he is doing it, the sounds that he is creating underscore how ridiculous Branwell's posing is. His archaic and convoluted syntax, 'To haste your love to me by fate delayed', has the same ridiculing effect. Besides his not being aware that Dorcas was already married to another goose, George, the most damning evidence of Branwell's self-absorbed insincerity is the ring he offers to Dorcas: it is actually a gift that Mopsus had given to Branwell. Mopsus, far from acting 'bland correct and rational', is outraged by Branwell's perfidy, and slugs him, saying 'Take that now you faithless thwarted changer!' Just before utter mayhem breaks out, the poem pauses to compose a verbal emblem complete with a moral and an allusion to the swan that only sings when it is dying, the central element of the Company of Musicians' coat of arms, as mentioned in *A Suit of Nettles*' 'I' epigraph. Here is the passage, following Mopsus's roughing up Branwell:

> Down to that dungy strawy chamber's floor
> Poor Branwell fell and got some kicks from George.
> Dorcas waddled up upon his form there
> And did the moral of it sweetly forge:
>
> DORCAS
> Beneath me girls you see a dying swan;
> Beside me view a goose: which race would you breed on?

With Dorcas's clever inversion of the 'Ugly Duckling' story, Branwell's humiliation is complete. Even George the goose, a 'chop-the-harp and fish-with-the-strings sort of oaf', is preferable to Branwell, a deluded Apollo wannabe, fittingly emblematized by Dorcas as a 'dying swan'. This pause to compose an emblem ends abruptly when Mopsus's loyalty to Branwell resurfaces, and he attacks the posing Dorcas. A brawl occurs, involving all of the geese. George and his 'big stout hot gander mob' get the best of it at first, but then Raymond, another poet goose, and member of Mopsus's crowd, takes over:

> But soon past pan, past tub, past trough George ran
> Chased by Raymond a goose for blood athirst,
> A goose who longed to see George in a hearse.
> Three times he chased poor George round the mash trough,
> Shouting vengeance on those who hated verse.

This eclogue's satiric medley of styles thus includes these raucous rhythms and rhymes that again ridicule the tendency to lose touch with reality by becoming caught up in pretentiousness regarding poetry. While the geese's battle is interrupted by the farmer, Ann, who comes to collect eggs and feed her gaggle, this energetic poetry indicates that now, at the close of the February eclogue, the battle might have temporarily stopped, but the tension persists.

The 'Farm' emblem evokes many more situations in *A Suit of Nettles* where contraries exist unresolved, and in the tensions between the pairs of oppositions, form a series of energetic wholes, including

- Effie's tale in 'March' of the contentious doorknob and door
- the poetry contest between Valancy and Raymond in 'April'
- the forces of procreation and birth control in 'May'
- Branwell's battle with melancholy in 'June'
- contrasting education philosophies in 'July'
- approaches to literary criticism in 'August'
- in 'September', at Mome Fair, Canadian history imagined as scenes from Dante's *Inferno,* followed by the history of Western philosophy with its various disagreements

- in 'October', Branwell's self-inflicted agony over Dorcas, paralleled by Raymond with the oncoming fall
- different ways to understand time, debated in 'November'
- the Christmas geese slaughter in 'December'.

Like 'The Farm', each of the twelve eclogues, and so the entirety of *A Suit of Nettles,* is animated by these ongoing dynamic oppositions. In counterpoint to these lively sets of attractions and resistances is the cycle of months and seasons that governs the overall movement of *A Suit of Nettles.*

As we might expect, the final selection of *A Suit of Nettles,* 'December', reveals numerous signs that the end of one year is the beginning of another, death the beginning of renewed life. The serenely resigned Effie comments, quoting *The Shepheardes Calender* ('November') that '"Death's the green pathway" to the fields of Life/"Die would we daily once it to expert."' (The verb 'to expert' in Spenser's era could mean 'to experience'.) Unlike Effie, Branwell is not ready to let himself be killed in anticipation of a new life; for this major character, the wearer of the suit of nettles, the annual cycle of nature will continue. The final dialogue of these two geese constitutes a riddle. Trying to dissuade Branwell from continuing in the hellish circles of history and philosophy that they discovered at Mome Fair, Effie says,

> Life inside of that is a crazed prison
> Of despair. You can't possibly want it.
>
> BRANWELL
> I can't help it, I'm afraid, I want the ring.
> I can't see a path that leads between one's
> Head & one's body.
>
> EFFIE
> When you are changed then
> One arm may always remain a goose wing.

The ring Branwell wants is the band that the farmers use to mark the geese that will not be slaughtered; it also represents the repetitive round of life in death that we often mistake for living. Effie's puzzling final remark refers to the Grimms' tale of 'The Six Swans' — not geese! — which tells of the transformation of six brothers into swans and back again to people. The transformation of one of the swans is not fully successful, so one brother is left with a swan's wing for an arm. Effie is indicating to Branwell that he is correct; he is not ready for the complete transformation that death brings. However, he has changed considerably, perhaps as much as one can hope for at any one time.

A Suit of Nettles leaves the geese at this point on Christmas Day, for the farmhouse, where the people feast on 'two roast geese at least', then go to bed on their 'fatter featherticks', also courtesy of the geese. As Ann and Peter sleep, Reaney again interpolates the world of fable, with the line 'Mother Holl shook down feathers from the sky', meaning that it snowed. This expression is originally from Hesse in central Germany (the birthplace of Reaney's maternal grandmother). The feather metaphor alludes to a fable about 'Mother Holle', as it is usually spelled. On one level, Reaney's mingling of these stories, including the Christmas story, contributes to the change of key that is occurring here at the end of *A Suit of Nettles*: moving from the goosehouse to the farmhouse and beyond. These stories emphasize too how we are able to live, and do live, according to stories that we tell ourselves. After Branwell's courtly lover's pose of being suicidal because of his unrequited love for Dorcas, his desire to go on living at the end of *A Suit of Nettles* shows his new self-understanding, a fresh awareness brought about by the multi-levelled action of the poem. Again like *One-man Masque* and 'The Farm', *A Suit of Nettles* reveals the potential for transcendence to be generated out of people's — and in this case, geese's — conflicts.

The next emblem, 'Egypt', generates insights into further aspects of Reaney's working with contraries, this time in a setting that is remote from 'The Farm'.

---

1. Further insight into the Little Lakes neighbourhood feuding can be found, slightly fictionalized, in 'The Ditch' stories in *The Box Social and Other Stories*.

2. Text quoted from the *Dictionary of Phrase and Fable* by E. Cobham Brewer, 1894. It refers to the sign of a London tavern, one of the first meeting places for Freemasons. The Company of Musicians also met there; the sign is a possibly joking diminution of their coat of arms, from a swan to a goose, from a lyre to a gridiron.

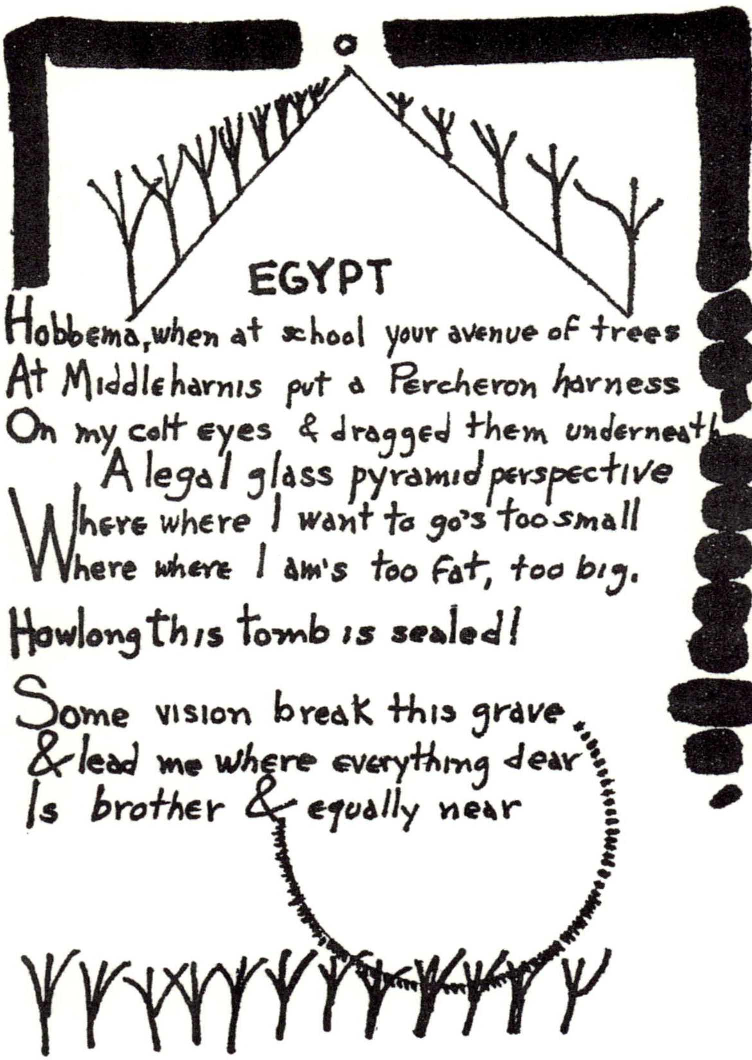
EGYPT
Hobbema, when at school your avenue of trees
At Middleharnis put a Percheron harness
On my colt eyes & dragged them underneath
A legal glass pyramid perspective
Where where I want to go's too small
Where where I am's too fat, too big.
Howlong this tomb is sealed!
Some vision break this grave
& lead me where everything dear
Is brother & equally near

Egypt

This emblem is both a complaint about the poet's and the readers' vision as it has been narrowed by being schooled in perspectival technique, and a demonstration of how things might appear in a less restricted world. With 'Egypt' Reaney is exploring an aspect of William Blake's concerns expressed in *The Marriage of Heaven and Hell.* In Plate 14 of that illustrated poem, Blake writes:

> If the doors of perception were cleansed every thing would appear to man as it is: infinite.
>
> For man has closed himself up, till he sees all things thro' narrow chinks of his cavern. (n.p.)

One determinant of these 'narrow chinks' is perspective, the topic of 'Egypt'.

In 1994 James Elkins published his study, *The Poetics of Perspective.* After struggling with the history and other complexities of the concept of perspective for nearly three hundred pages, he concludes with these rather poignant words:

> I have tried throughout the text to 'step back' and say something 'outside' of perspective's regimens. I have found it extremely difficult to preserve even the illusion that I might be doing so.
>
> And so the best way to end may be to acknowledge the persistent pull of perspective. Perspective directs our eyes and orders our thoughts.... Perspective seems to control not only what I see — it sets the conditions of visibility — but how I see and how I describe the way I see. (272)

Elkins's inability to gain a satisfactory take on his subject results in part

from his realization that perspective is not only an artist's technique, but also a common metaphor. And in Elkins's case, much the same dilemma as that expressed by Reaney's 'Egypt' emblem, perspective's metaphorical control is actually blinding him. Oddly, perhaps, but congruently with the complaint in Reaney's 'Egypt' emblem, perspective as a metaphor signals people's separateness from one another, their 'individual perspectives', while perspective as a factor in pictures tends to unify our perceptions to the extent of becoming overwhelmingly ideological — the point of view specified by the picture is *the* way to interpret the subject.

In his article 'Vision in Canada?' Reaney comments directly on perspective's pernicious influence and how to overcome it:

> Margaret Avison's 'Perspective' poem battles vigorously with that beloved idol of our drawing classes — 'perspective'. I suppose it may have crossed your mind when asked in grade 4 to draw a railway showing perspective (surely a doleful exercise for children who do not see reality that way) that in reality the railway tracks never do join; otherwise, as Avison points out, you'd never get to Ottawa. If you now look at the tracks and imagine that you see that they never join, you become a gigantic person capable of such a feat and also make a visionary correction of our world as viewed by tedious photographic realism.... (944–45)

Reaney goes on to exclaim, in parallel with the text of 'Egypt', 'We'd have a lot more Picassos in Ontario art if we'd just stop saying: "Draw a railway in perspective"' (945). When we were taught to draw railway tracks as meeting at a point, our world views shrank and were subjected to artificial limits. This analysis of perspective explains for readers of Reaney's emblems a good deal about the emblems' style. They require their readers to 'make a visionary correction', and to see the world, in Blake's word, as 'infinite'.

The opening six lines of the text of 'Egypt' are addressed to Meindert Hobbema (1638–1709), the Dutch Baroque-era landscape painter. Hobbema's masterpiece is *The Avenue at Middelharnis* (1689), much admired for its treatment of perspective, which creates centres of interest in the back- and middle ground, as well as in the foreground. In his copy of an Ontario Department of Education art manual (see page 178), Reaney annotated a discussion of this painting as an example of the technique of perspective with the words 'my peinture favori'.[1] Perspective

Meinert Hobbema, *The Avenue at Middelharnis* (1689).
(Courtesy of the National Gallery, London, England.)

has been explored since classical Greek times, when Euclid (c. 300 BCE) devised his laws of optics. The modern geometrical theory of perspective was advanced in the early fifteenth century; perspective became a fundamental scheme informing Renaissance art. Following a demonstration of the use of perspective in painting by Filippo Brunelleschi (1377–1446) in Florence in 1425, the technique caught on, and was adopted by most European painters, and is in use to this day.[2]

The picture at the top of Reaney's 'Egypt' parodies Hobbema's painting, as Reaney's text puns on the name of the town, Middel*harnis* and a horse's *harness*, the metaphorical restriction on the schoolboy's eyes. The phrase 'legal glass pyramid perspective' evokes the culturally binding, normative function of perspective's rules, and also creates overlapping visual images of a magnifier on a lawyer's desk, as well as the converging-railway-tracks, and in this case, the converging-lines-of-trees shape of those famous Egyptian monuments. The roofs of the houses on the right also suggest pyramids.[3] For the well-tutored schoolboy, the effect of perspective's laws is to distort his infinite and accurate vision, and ultimately to diminish his own human potential. The laws of perspective, for example, stipulate that we perceive things solely from a single point of view: the place from which our eyes see, closing down the imaginative possibilities of vision in a normally subliminal way. In Reaney's line 'How long this tomb is sealed!' the poet cleverly conflates the pyramid as a tomb and a geometrical shape with his own death-like entrapment within the restrictive laws of perspective.

By metaphorical extension, 'perspective' refers not only to the visual, but to concepts of all kinds. Blake's 'narrow chinks' are also systems of thought — such as Euclidean geometry, the rules of logic, church dogma, and Newtonian physics — which, instead of enlarging people's perspectives, shut them down, like railway tracks which meet. The final three lines of the emblem's text pray for release both from the harness of perspective by which people in Western cultures are restricted, and also from the isolation imposed by our individual perspectives. Like the 'Farm' emblem, 'Egypt' illustrates this liberation graphically. By means of two drawings, 'Egypt' establishes magnetic poles that generate the emblem's textual lines of force — 'Egypt' is figuratively a bar magnet, while 'The Farm' is a horseshoe magnet.

The small circle at the top of the 'Egypt' emblem appears again

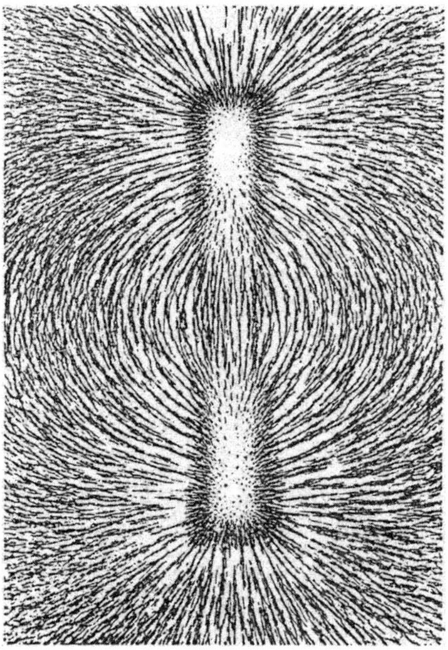

Bar Magnet, showing lines of force, comparable to those of the emblem 'Egypt'.

at the bottom, much enlarged, so that we can see little rays on the circumference, not a series of railway ties receding into an imaginary point somewhere behind the frame, but 'equally near'. Similarly, whereas in the part of the emblem above the words, the trees, like Hobbema's, diminish into the distance as prescribed by the convention of perspectival drawing, and in doing so outline a pyramid shape, in the bottom part of the emblem the trees are lined up, as if each were equidistant from the viewer. With both of the bottom images, the circle and the line of trees, the implied point of view is open: no matter where the viewer might be located, the images would appear as they do in the emblem. The viewer is thus no longer restricted by seeing 'all things thro' narrow chinks of his cavern', in Blake's words, and is released from the 'grave' / 'pyramid' in Reaney's terms.

As noted in connection with 'The Farm', Blake associates bricks and brick-making, and thus the Pyramids, with the Israelites' death-in-life state of confinement in Egypt, as described in the Bible's Book of Exodus. Northrop Frye clarifies Blake's symbolism as being based not only on the bondage aspect of the Jews' situation, but also on Egypt's being, in Blake's estimation, the 'final decadence' of African culture, 'with its hieratic ritual, oppressive priestly code, tyrannical monarchy and the "mathematic form" of its pyramids' (*Fearful Symmetry* 130). Using brick-making imagery to elaborate on the Egyptian captivity, Blake writes in *Jerusalem* that people's souls were 'bak'd/In bricks to build the pyramids of Heber & Terah' (656). Two of Blake's visual images also include pyramid shapes, with damning intentions regarding perspective that are similar to Reaney's in 'Egypt'. Blake's famous portrait of Sir Isaac Newton could be an illustration for the verbal image in 'Egypt', 'A legal glass pyramid perspective'. Blake's colour print shows the great lawmaker of physics forming a pyramid with his compasses and the lines on the scroll. Seated on a rocky outcropping that verges on dark nothingness, Newton is measuring and arbitrarily establishing mathematical proportions to translate the universe's living forms into abstract numbers and ratios. The harnessing of the colt's eyes in the 'Egypt' emblem is a characteristic of this perverted process, as demonstrated by the poet's being distracted by the rules of perspective into relativistic thinking, rather than seeing things for what they are. Being subject to 'legal glass pyramid perspective', is to be

> Where where I want to go's too small
> Where where I am's too fat, too big.

William Blake, *Newton* (1795).
(Courtesy of the Tate Gallery, London, England.)

In *Newton,* the rock on which the scientist sits is a death symbol, related by Blake to the rock that Jesus had to push away from the mouth of the tomb where he was buried. For the 'Egypt' poet's rebirth, the seal on the tomb of perspective must be broken. He implores, 'Some vision break this grave.' Two of Reaney's poems in particular, along with Blake's and Frye's ideas, can help us to realize the meanings of 'vision' when they are brought near the magnetic field of 'Egypt'. We'll start with some basic considerations about 'vision' as it pertains to eyesight, then move on to metaphorical aspects of the word.

Even when 'vision' simply refers to physical eyesight, the term is not as simple as it might seem. Central to our concern with Reaney's 'Egypt' emblem is Blake's analysis of John Locke's model of 'human understanding'. Locke (1632–1704), Newton and Sir Francis Bacon (1561–1626) constituted for Blake an evil triumvirate because of the harmful effects on people of their shared approach to the nature of knowledge. The three influential scientists' epistemology is empiricist; they believe that all or most of our knowledge derives from sensory experiences. In Blake's view, Locke, like Newton, sucked the life out of the world by abstracting principles from things. Newton's abstraction is mathematical and geometrical, overlaying such patterns on things, and treating the patterns as the reality; Locke's abstraction separates 'sensations', or perceptions, from 'reflections' on them, categorizing sensations and turning them into abstract 'ideas' and patterns of generalizations, all in order to explain how we conceptualize and thus control the chaos of our sensory experiences. This control, of course, is illusory.

Blake, on the other hand, ignoring many of the subtleties of these scientists' thought (as I have just done), judged these descriptions to be degenerate and pernicious, and held that distinct perception is far superior to consolidating a bunch of faint memories. 'All Knowledge is Particular,' he declares. Frye summarizes Blake's analysis:

> Reflection on sensation is concerned only with the mere memory of the sensation, and Blake always refers to Locke's reflection as 'memory'. Memory of an image must always be less than the perception of an image. Just as it is impossible to do a portrait from memory as well as from life, so it is impossible for an abstract idea

> to be anything more than a subtracted idea, a vague and hazy afterimage. (*Fearful Symmetry* 15)

Instead of this debilitating process, Blake believes that the senses do not produce images for the mind to reflect upon, but that the mind energetically creates images or what he calls 'forms', out of the data that the senses supply. 'Perception, then,' Frye writes, 'is not something we do with our senses; it is a mental act.' The words 'do' and 'act' accentuate the point that perception is not passive reception. The mental activity of perception is the imagination's work, the dynamic making of images; and, Frye goes on, '"imagination" is the regular term used by Blake to denote man as an acting and perceiving being. That is, a man's imagination is his life' (*Fearful Symmetry* 19). One of the political consequences of people's submitting to such restrictions as that symbolized by perspective in 'Egypt' is, in Blake's analysis, tyranny, a state that eventuates from the citizenry's being passive (*Fearful Symmetry* 190).

As Blake knew, his philosophical position has much in common with the idealism of one of Blake's contemporaries, the Irish thinker Bishop George Berkeley (1685–1753). Non-specialists would recognize the riddle associated with Berkeley (but not formulated by him in these words), 'If a tree falls in a forest, and no one is there to hear it, does it make a sound?' Ian Tipton, author of *Berkeley: The Philosophy of Immaterialism*, explains,

> when we — ordinary men and women — talk of houses, mountains, rivers and so on, we are talking about what we experience or are aware of, not of occult objects that we are not directly aware of at all. It follows, or at least it seemed to Berkeley to follow, that if when we refer to houses, mountains and rivers we are referring to things we are aware of, and if (as other philosophers agreed) we are aware only of ideas, houses, mountains and rivers must *be* 'ideas' or appearances or, better, 'collections' of such ideas. Certainly — and this was one thing that his readers found most difficult to handle, but which Berkeley himself was most insistent on — there is no need to deny that houses, mountains and rivers exist, but only to stress (common-sensibly) that they are the very things we perceive,

> which is to say that they are mind-dependent ideas. Their *esse* (being) is *percipi* (to be perceived); they exist only in the mind. (Tipton)

On this point Frye comments that 'The acceptance of the *esse-est-percipi* principle unites the subject and the object. By introducing the idea of "reflection" we separate them again' (*Fearful Symmetry* 16–17). To thinkers such as Blake and Reaney, this unifying of the subject/object dichotomy is crucial, since the overarching purpose of their artistic projects is through imagination to recreate in human form the chaotic, fallen world in which we live — to make our desired world alive in us.

Reaney's 1961 poem 'To Bishop Berkeley' particularizes the philosopher's 'to be is to be perceived', '*esse est percipi*', primarily with visual images.

> How beautiful the barnyard is,
> The little flashlight says.
> Wherever I look is shining
> And active as plays.
>
> So says the lamp within the house
> At golden plaster, golden walls
> And candles remark how wainscot
> Gleams like calls.
>
> Even the urinal match said,
> Oh what beautiful hands
> And the oozy willow-the-wisp
> Marvelled blue quicksands.
>
> Oh Wordsworth and nature-walkers
> Thy nature barnyard is;
> Her trees are plaster, wainscot hills,
> Handy vale and miry mess.
>
> Wherever walks your lantern self
> The crop of wonder then sprouts up;

Five kinds of music,
The spear of time, the spatial cup. (*Poems* 187)

In common with Reaney's 'Egypt' emblem, this poem is a meditation on perspective. 'To Bishop Berkeley' imagines a play-box of possibilities for perception if it were freed from the limitations of conventional perspective. The poem inhabits the points of view of a flashlight, a lamp, a match, a 'willow-the-wisp', and the 'lantern self' voices of the poem. These lights bring various things to life, make them 'Active as plays'. This striking comparison shows the poet acting as a 'literalist of the imagination' by stressing the role of 'plays', a type of verbal art, in recreating the fallen world. Similarly transformative, through the power of language, is the word 'beautiful' in reference to a barnyard. Such livestock enclosures are not usually all that pretty, but here a barnyard is linguistically changed by being named 'beautiful'.

The second stanza conjures another image that disregards the narrowing effects of perspective and reveals perception's unifying powers: the lamp, the perceiver, admires the plaster walls which, along with the lamp, are actively shining. The poem does not attribute causality regarding the shining of any of these things, it overtly brings them together. Imposing a cause/effect system to interpret events is a Lockean, Newtonian error that leads back to temporality, away from infinite vision. The candles' simile, saying that the 'wainscot/Gleams like calls' makes a leap that according to our everyday frames of reference seems impossible: what does gleaming have to do with calling? The riddling comparison tells us that as calls are actions, so, in an imaginatively recreated world, is gleaming. Gleaming is not an abstract quality of the wainscot, somehow separate from it; rather, gleaming is what the wainscot is doing.

The third stanza's first two lines, in which answering the call of nature is illuminated by a match, indicate that not only do things come to be by being perceived, but people do too. The subject/object dichotomy dissolves. The match illuminates the hands of someone's body, signifying that this someone is both perceived and perceiver. Frye explains how this idea relates to Berkeley's thought:

> Berkeley draws a distinction … between the ideas we have of the

> existence of other things and the 'notion' we have of our own existence. We know that we are a reality beyond others' perceptions of us, and that if *esse est percipi*, then *esse est percipere* as well. (*Fearful Symmetry* 18)

The emphasis here, as in 'To Bishop Berkeley', is on both: 'to be is to be perceived', and also 'to be is to perceive'. These two aspects of being are activities, not states, and people are free to use their imaginative energies to realize and to be realized by the world that they desire. 'Will-o'-the-wisp' is the folk name for '*ignis fatuus*', the phosphorescence sometimes observed hovering over swamps, and meaning figuratively 'a thing (rarely a person) that deludes or misleads by means of fugitive appearances' ('*Ignis fatuus*' and 'Will o' the wisp'). So the 'willow-the-wisp', as Reaney spells it in 'To Bishop Berkeley', is another illuminator, elusive and mirage-like, that brings to being and transmutes, marvellously, the quicksands.

'Wordsworth' in stanza four is William Wordsworth (1770–1850), a contemporary of Blake's. He was a Romantic poet who became England's poet laureate. Blake admired his poetry to some extent. 'To Bishop Berkeley' characterizes Wordsworth as one of several 'nature walkers' because he and his sister Dorothy, as well as Samuel Taylor Coleridge (1772–1834) walked, talked and composed poetry in England's Lake District. Wordsworth believed in an organic bond between people and the natural world, going almost to the extent of pantheism in holding that nature is an emblem of God's mind. To all of these dichotomies in Wordsworth's thinking — people/nature, people/God, nature/God — 'To Bishop Berkeley' supplies some Blakean corrective lenses. Instead of placing nature on a pedestal — Wordsworth, for instance, says in 'Tintern Abbey' that he is a 'worshipper of Nature' — the poem advises that 'Thy nature barnyard is.' No doubt Reaney was grinning when he wrote this metaphoric reminder that cow manure is part of nature, but the lines mean more: nature is not exclusively rivers and trees 'out there' in some pristine location; nature is created by being perceived, so it is human in form, 'barnyard nature', as well as inside the imagined imaginer.

Also important to note, the poem's figurative language has moved from similes to metaphors. Frye explains that similes compare two distinct things, whereas metaphors unite, or in Blake's terms, 'identify' their elements (*Fearful Symmetry* 116–17). The identifying of subject and object works on this level also. The features of 'nature barnyard' also incorporate in metaphors the lighted things from the previous three stanzas of 'To Bishop Berkeley': 'trees are plaster', golden; 'wainscot hills', covered in woods; 'Handy vale', both the urinal — always handy when needed! — and the Romantic Wordsworthian word for a nearby valley; and 'miry mess', the quicksands swamp.

The final stanza brings together the 'plays' of the first four stanzas, and lets us readers know what we have already suspected, that not only Wordsworth, but all of us are 'nature-walkers' whose selves, in perceiving our world, bring it to light. The second line's farming metaphor, akin to the 'nature barnyard is' metaphor, indicates again that the imagination's work is to humanize nature. The 'crop of wonder' is music, the 'spear of time', and 'the spatial cup'. Music transposes the poem from the visual to the aural domain, implying that not only vision, but also our other senses have roles to play in recreating the fallen world. Time-as-spear and space-as-cup work symbolically to suggest an apocalyptic union, the spear being a male shape, the cup being female.

By bringing 'To Bishop Berkeley' into the meaning field of the 'Egypt' emblem, it is evident that the 'vision' sought in the emblem and realized in the poem is imaginative as well as corporeal. Vision is both at once. Also, again simultaneously, we see with this poem and this emblem the following principle stated by Frye:

> The product of imaginative life is most clearly seen in the work of art, which is a unified mental vision of experience. (*Fearful Symmetry* 24)

So far we have explored through 'Egypt' and 'To Bishop Berkeley' various operations of vision when it is freed of conventional restraints. But in addition to the liberation experience elicited by 'To Bishop Berkeley', there is also in 'Egypt' a good deal of concern with the consequences of restricted vision. What is it like inside the pyramid tomb of 'Egypt'? We need not dwell on this situation long since most of us inhabit this desecrated world on a daily basis. Briefly, one could sum it up by quoting the opinion of the English philosopher Thomas Hobbes (1588–1679) on what life would be like in the state of nature, with no rules and regulations. It would be war, and life would be 'solitary, poore, nasty, brutish, and short' (*Leviathan* ch. 13, para. 9). The shorthand term used by both Blake and Reaney is 'fallen'.

However, Reaney, in tune with Blake, never rests in this frame of mind, as our exploration of 'Egypt' and 'To Bishop Berkeley' has demonstrated. The emblem vividly establishes the perspective situation as a pyramid-shaped tomb and a harness on the poet's eyes, then proceeds to transform this limited sight into infinite vision. The startling imagery of 'To Bishop Berkeley' and the direct address to 'Wordsworth and nature-walkers' awaken the poem's readers to the reality of this vision, helping us to imagine a world without the imposed perspective of such divisions as subject/object, active/passive.

Underpinning this artistic strategy that occurs nearly always in Reaney's works is Blake's discriminating between 'contraries' and 'negations'. As we shall see in connection with Reaney's 'The Riddle', Blake favours clarity of outline in painting, rather than the kind of blurriness in his contemporary and artistic rival J.M.W. Turner's work. (Significantly, considering the links between 'Egypt' and Blake's ideas, Turner [1775–1851] was the Professor of Perspective at the Royal Academy in London for thirty years, from 1807 to 1837.) Similarly, Blake insists that in the search for truth in words, forthrightly defined error is preferable to vague expressions of error, whether caused by hypocrisy or even well-intentioned self-deception. Frye quotes the Proverb of Hell, Plate 10 of *The Marriage of Heaven and Hell*, which expresses Blake's principle: 'Truth can never be told so as to be understood, and not be believ'd' (*Fearful Symmetry* 188). Frye continues,

> The idea that truth in a false context is worse than outspoken falsehood leads in Blake's thought to a distinction between a 'contrary' and a 'negation..... Blake and Locke are contraries: both feel that imagination, liberty and life are in their systems, and they must clash or we shall never know who is right. Hobbes is a negation: he cares too little for imagination or liberty to clash with any defender of it.... The clash of contraries is thus an essential part of the 'redemption' of mankind. (188–89)

In his work Reaney uses Blake's insight as a basis on which to create in the reader or audience the experience of 'redemption' or, in less religious-sounding terms, the realization that there are possibilities all around us to fulfil our desires to make the world more human.

To conclude this chapter, let's see how perspective works in several more of Reaney's works in which pyramids appear.

There are two versions of a 'family tree pyramid' in *Colours in the Dark,*) one apex up (▲), the other base up (▼) (34 and 128). These pattern poems are performed by the actors both aurally and visually. The pyramids are an intriguing way to think about time, and their pyramid shape also opens the spatial dimension. With the symbolism of the pyramid in mind, it is easy to recognize how these two tombs of perception sealed by the conventions of time and space make up the contrary that generates the 'One child' who emerges at the end of *Colours in the Dark.* In the play, the Kids call out that 'it takes a lot of people to produce one child' (34). They then '*form a family tree pyramid*' on stage, as well as call out the following:

It takes
Two parents
Four Grandparents
Eight Great grandparents
Sixteen Great great grandparents
Thirty-two Great great great grandparents
Sixty-four Great great great great grandparents
One hundred and twenty-eight Great great great great great grandparents
Two hundred and fifty-six Great great great great great great grandparents
Five hundred and twelve Great great great great great great great grandparents
One thousand and twenty-four Great great great great great great great great grandparents

The primary characteristic of the living-death state that this pyramid poem emphasizes is the burden of temporality that people bear in the fallen world. As perspective harnesses our vision, so time regulates our lives by arbitrary units.

The pyramid shape recurs as an emblematic feature of the play, the second time being an analogue of the previous, apex-up pyramid, using natural objects instead of family members (65).

EGYPT

It takes
The Remembering
Of four seasons
Eight Stars
Sixteen Sunsets
Thirty-two Wind whistles
Sixty-four Dewdrops in the sunrise
One hundred and twenty-eight Trembling leaves
Two hundred and fifty-six Pebbles
Five hundred and twelve Snowflakes
One thousand and twenty-four Cloud shadows
To make one soul

Some of the natural objects here are mentioned also in the play's finale, the poem 'Gifts', recited just after the third pyramid has formed. In this 'remembering' pyramid remembering suggests a process of reassembling the person's fallen, scattered body parts, as the Egyptian Isis did with her brother/husband Osiris. The natural things to be remembered suggest, as does 'To Bishop Berkeley', that in an infinite, redeemed world, the human being is both imaginer of and imagined by that world. Here is the third pyramid, an inverted version of the first:

1024 great great great great great great great great grandparents
512 great great great great great great great grandparents
256 great great great great great great grandparents
128 great great great great great grandparents
64 great great great great grandparents
32 great great great grandparents
16 great great grandparents
8 great grandparents
4 grandparents
2 parents
One child.

Thematically, the three pyramids build by contraries to the release of the 'all-containing child', in Terry Griggs's phrase (19). Structurally, the three pyramids develop the contraries/liberation theme as recurring essentially musical motifs that culminate with the re-born 'one child'. Readers must imagine the striking changes in colours and seasons and moods of an actual performance of *Colours in the Dark* to appreciate the powerful sense of recognition that an audience experiences as the play is enacted. Nevertheless, reading *Colours in the Dark* or watching and listening, we are offered the opportunity to release ourselves from the fallen perspective.

The closing three lines of the 'Egypt' emblem are both a prayer for 'vision' and an intuitive conception of the world as it would be, reborn into freedom from the perspective harness pyramid-grave. The words 'dear' and 'brother' indicate that in the recreated world love would be present and fundamental. As Frye summarizes,

> Love, or the transformation of the objective into the beloved, and art, or the transformation of the object into the created, are the two activities pursued on this earth to repair the damage of the Fall.... (*Fearful Symmetry* 126)

The words 'dear' and 'brother' also make the final word, 'near', into a pun: 'equally near' anticipates a world where affection is not corrupted into the hierarchies of tyranny and warfare; and they simultaneously refer to the way things would appear unfettered by the strictures of conventional perspective.

The next emblem we shall consider, 'Within Within', also longs for release: like 'Egypt', it envisions a way out.

---

1. This copy of the art manual is in the collection of James S. Reaney and Susan Wallace. Thanks to Susan for pointing out this annotation.

2. Edgerton, as well as Elkins, presents an account of the nature and significance of the developments and use of perspective.

3. More clearly evident in the detail of the painting, at https://www.national-galleryimages.co.uk/.

Within Within

This emblem sets up a questioning relationship between the text and the visual images, and also between the emblem as a whole and the reader. Like 'Egypt', 'Within Within' is a meditation on vision and imagination. Reminiscent of the shapes in 'The Castle', the illustration consists of six different arrangements of a square, a triangle and a circle. Read from the top down, they form a complete series of different 'within within' statements, thus:

▲ within ■ within ●.
● within ▲ within ■.
■ within ● within ▲.
■ within ▲ within ●.
▲ within ● within ■.
● within ■ within ▲.

The text, meanwhile, is in counterpoint to these configurations, presenting various sensory images. Readers of 'Within Within' are offered the task of bringing the text's hypothetical interpretations together with the diagrams. As the text of 'Within Within' unfolds, the readers' reliance on conventions of pictorial realism becomes less and less tenable. The emblem pries us away from our learned, habitual methods of understanding art and jolts us into the realm of imagination.

The phrase 'In a man's eye a tear reflecting' could conceivably correspond pictorially to the top left dark circle enclosing a white square and triangle. More probably, the textual line serves as a warning that if this emblem is a match-up challenge, it might be trickier than expected. 'In a fish a face looks out': yes, I see it. Right beside that tall 'I' of the word 'In' is a square aquarium containing a triangular fish with a circular face inside it, looking out. That was easy enough. Now: 'The twilight elms

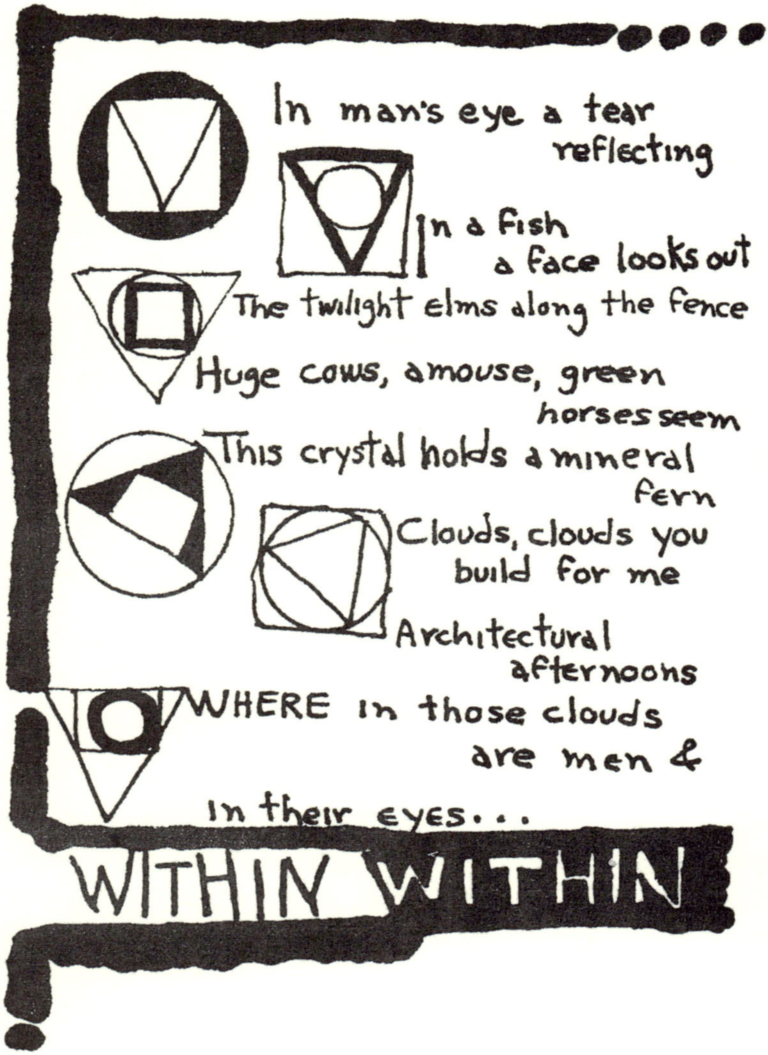
In man's eye a tear
reflecting
In a fish
a face looks out
The twilight elms along the fence
Huge cows, amouse, green
horses seem
This crystal holds a mineral
fern
Clouds, clouds you
build for me
Architectural
afternoons
WHERE in those clouds
are men &
in their eyes...
WITHIN WITHIN

along the fence.' Where are they? 'Huge cows, a mouse, green horses seem.' At this point, the relationship between the text and illustration has certainly moved out of the 'statement X-is-a-verbal-clue-to-help-spot-diagram-Y' mode. 'This crystal', though, might momentarily evoke a triangular prism. Looking into and through a prism does create a new view of things. Reading the lines, 'Clouds, clouds you build for me/Architectural afternoons', might suggest that the six variations on circle/square/triangle are the wind-blown clouds, out of whose moving shapes the poet's mind generates verbal images. Reaney's poems 'Clouds' and 'The Clouds' from *The Red Heart* similarly enact this generative process.

The ending of the emblem's text is a question which answers itself. Not only does it collapse this scientific subject-object paradigm, but the division between text and illustration collapses too. Isn't the first word of the textual question the 'O' within the diagram of the square within the triangle? 'O WHERE in those clouds/are men &/in their eye.... WITHIN WITHIN.' The movement of this emblem, including the formal uniting of the text and the images, is to empower readers to see with our imaginative eyes. In 'Search for an Undiscovered Alphabet', Reaney reports his discovery that 'the first letter in an alphabet of diagrams would have to be a simplification of the human eye — that is, a circle with a central dot' (39). He concludes this article by emphasizing the importance of a truly human point of view, and in the process, stating the theme of 'Within Within': 'If the iris and pupil of the human eye are indeed the first letter of this alphabet we perhaps have an explanation for the peculiar effectiveness of designs and diagrams. We like to see things with our own eyes' (41). Keeping in mind this theme of empowering readers to see with our own eyes, let's suppress the urge to expect representational realism from this emblem, and reconsider it as a magnetic pole in the context of some other works that it draws into its force field. The word 'within' first calls for attention.

Reaney's 'To Sunday School', part of a series of poems dated 1964, describes the young poet's walk to church with his parents. They travel a path through meadows, near a forest and marshland, and, suddenly,

> Here is Cousin Tommy's field of peas,
> Fifteen acres of cool green involved

Succulence; were it not that we'd break
Several commandments we'd stay and eat at our ease.

Temptation successfully avoided, by the time the young boy arrives at church, he exclaims,

Oh Sunday walk of plants and animals!
From thy green fars and golden nearnesses
I've learnt already the Sunday School lesson:
That Earth may lie within Heaven's walls. (*Poems* 195)

This possible location for Earth, 'within Heaven's walls', is the poem's revelation. The poet experiences from both far and near the delights of nature, and these perspectives collapse into the realization not that Heaven is in Earth, but that 'Earth may lie within Heaven's walls.' That is, in Blakean terms, the boy's perceiving Nature, actively creating it in his mind, is a contribution to making the infinite heavenly city, in which nature has its existence, as do all imagined things. In terms of Reaney, as the poet who writes 'To Sunday School', Frye's statement is apposite: 'It is the function of art to illuminate the human form of nature' (*Fearful Symmetry* 123).

The closing line of the text of 'Within Within' might indicate such a triumphal epiphany, but the opening lines say otherwise:

In man's eye a tear reflecting
In a fish a face looks out

The tear is not a tear of joy; it is 'reflecting', sadly, in the passive way that we noted while exploring the 'Egypt' emblem. Reflection, as Blake understands Locke's concept, is passive, and leads to abstractions. For Blake, distinct, active perceptions are far superior to Lockean reflections. The 'face' looking out of a fish in the second line belongs to the biblical prophet Jonah, who was saved from drowning during a tempest at sea by a great fish that the god Jehovah had prepared for that purpose. In comparison with Jonah's earlier life of disobeying the Hebrews' god's orders, and therefore being 'afflicted' and living 'in the belly of hell', Jonah realized that surviving there in the storm-free belly of the fish he was in relatively good shape, to the point of his actually being thankful, and vowing to follow Jehovah's instructions in future. After three days and three nights, 'the Lord spake unto the fish, and it vomited out Jonah upon the dry land' (2.10). In Reaney's emblem 'Within Within' we find Jonah still inside the fish, however, not yet knowing how his predicament will turn out. Jonah comments repentantly in his prayers to Jehovah that 'I am cast out of thy sight; yet I will look again toward thy holy temple' (2.4). The first of Jonah's visual metaphors indicates his god's displeasure, the second, Jonah's intention to mend his ways. It is a turning point in his life. The Bible story goes on to narrate how Jonah does accomplish the task that Jehovah had set for him, but at the end of the book he is again being chastised by Jehovah for second-guessing the god's behaviour. Setting aside the pleasurable black humour of this episode, for the purpose of interpreting 'Within Within' it is necessary to understand the exact state of the face that looks out. The person for whom the face stands in the emblem is stuck, almost dead, but about to experience a revival, though neither a complete nor a permanent redemption. This thematic trajectory is precisely parallel to that of the emblem.

From the face looking out of the fish, 'Within Within' next attends to several land images. 'The twilight elms along the fence' connote a transitional state, twilight, and still being restricted, systematized by the fence. From the verb 'seem' at the end of the fourth line, 'Huge cows, a mouse, green horses seem', we infer that the text's speaker is fantasizing, perhaps on the basis of the circle/square/triangle shapes. Reading on, we encounter 'Clouds', making it possible to connect the things that 'seem' with the clouds — clouds being marvellous shape-shifters that can fleetingly resemble twilight elms, a fence, cows, mice, horses, or anything else you choose.

'This crystal holds a mineral fern', the fifth line, is a riddle, and it works in a way similar to the preceding lines, with the poet's mind at play, creating human patterns out of nature. In this case, though, the created verbal image is less a matter of individual fancy, no matter how symbolically resonant it is, than publicly acknowledged. The word 'crystal' derives from the Greek word 'κρύσταλλος', meaning 'clear ice' ('crystal'). The emblem's 'crystal' could be a snowflake: 'Fernlike Stellar Dendrite' is a snowflake shape (Libbrecht), and snow is a mineral (Sheffield). So the clarification of the riddling line could well be 'snowflake'. The public

A Fernlike Stellar Dendrite Snowflake (Libbrecht).

quality of 'This crystal holds a mineral fern' — we all see patterns in snowflakes, — in contrast with the images that to the emblem's speaker merely 'seem' to exist, is worth stressing here because of the implied growth towards universal inclusiveness in the emblem's imaginings.

A snowflake is also a key image in *Fearful Symmetry's* fifth chapter, 'The Word Within the Word'. (As we'll see, this title's contiguity to the title 'Within Within' is the tip of the iceberg of fruitful interactions between Frye's chapter and Reaney's emblem.) Frye explains much the same theme in Blake's thought that 'Within Within' particularizes as art:

> In human society everything from the Sistine ceiling to thumbscrews owes its form to man's mind and character in one of its various aspects. Similarly the character of everything in nature expresses an aspect of the human mind. We say that a snowflake has a symmetrical design, not because the snowflake has consciously produced it, but because we can see the design. We see that the snowflake has achieved something of which we alone can see the form, and the form of the snowflake is therefore a human form. (*Fearful Symmetry* 123)

'This crystal holds a mineral fern' is a riddle because the emblem is reinforcing the theme articulated by Frye. Readers have to perceive the form within the line. As I have demonstrated, this perceiving is an action; we 'see the design'.

The sixth line of the text lets us know that the six triangle/square/circle shapes are metaphorically clouds; both the shapes and the clouds set a person's mind to creating images, just as architects create buildings out of simple shapes.

The emblem's climax begins in the next line, already noted, where the 'O' in the visual image fuses the visual image with the verbal sentence. They form a question, and that question portends a lack. A statement of Blake's, quoted by Frye in *Fearful Symmetry*, identifies Reaney's emblem's men in the clouds:

> Think of a white cloud as being holy, you cannot love it; but think of a holy man within the cloud, love springs up in your thoughts, for to think of holiness distinct from man is impossible to the affections. (Keynes, *Blake: Complete Writings* 90; *Fearful Symmetry* 125)

Should the emblem's speaker have been able not only to see the clouds, but to see men in the clouds, the imagining process would have been completed: the emblem would have thoroughly humanized nature. Instead, in the emblem's terms, the speaker remains within the fish, looking out. This pattern occurs in a number of Reaney's works, including, for example, the poem 'Jordan', dated 1956, which he wrote prior to reading *Fearful Symmetry*. Clearly, before he went to the University of Toronto Reaney had developed his understanding of ideas that he shares with Blake and Frye particularly. In 'Jordan' the poet sees clouds disappearing across the river and flying over the Promised Land; however, even replete with Bible knowledge, the poem's speaker is unable to experience fully the results of baptism, in other words, to cross the Jordan River. The clouds leave him behind. In the emblem he can see the 'within within' shapes and patterns, but not the revered men in the clouds who would hold out the potential for love. Love and art, as we observed in connection with the 'Egypt' emblem, are the two ways we have to improve our distorted world. Paradoxically, as a painstakingly, lovingly, created work of art, 'Within Within' does its fair share of this improving.

The central myth of Reaney's work is common to all literature, and, according to Frye, this myth is most fully elaborated by the Bible (*Fearful Symmetry* 108–9). 'Myth' here means a 'story', not a falsity. This myth is cyclic. Frye calls it 'the vision of this world as God sees it' (*Fearful Symmetry* 108). This is a diagram of the myth. With this pattern in mind, it

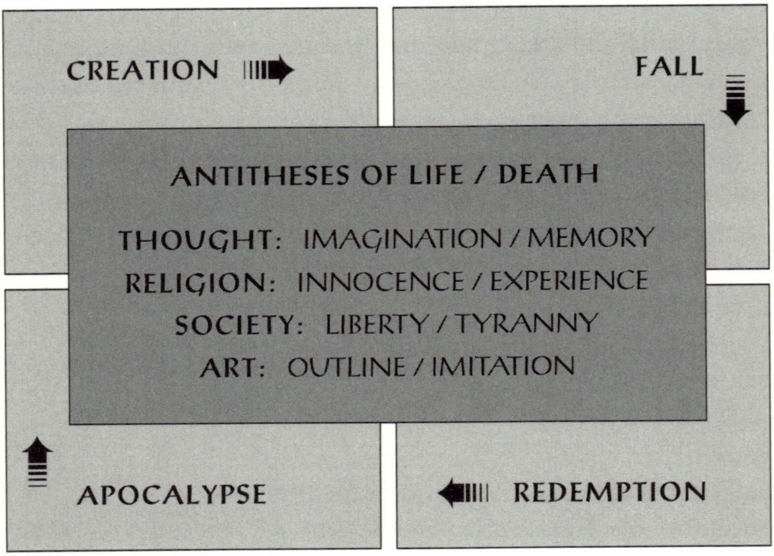

becomes easier to locate works of art in terms of the myth. Most works other than the Bible do not attempt to encompass the entire vision, but rather to articulate a portion of the cycle. The antitheses around which these states revolve are thematic, indicators of the struggles taking place. Reaney's emblem 'Within Within', as we have seen, seeks a complete vision but does not achieve it. We could place it somewhere close to the line between 'Redemption' and 'Apocalypse', on the 'Redemption' side. 'Jordan' would occupy a similar position. 'To Sunday School', though, with its learned lesson, 'That Earth may lie within Heaven's walls', seems apocalyptic. Another poem of Reaney's that is drawn into the force field of 'Within Within' occupies a third location in the cycle. 'Dream Within Dream', is an early poem, published in *The Red Heart* in 1949. As the poem's title indicates, it too plays with the notion of 'within'. Unlike the emblem's striving for a complete vision, 'Dream Within Dream' presents a series of nightmares in which the sense of 'within' is a panicked descent into a deeper and deeper sleep.

Dream Within Dream

I slept and dreamed
A collection of dreams

That fitted each into each other
Like the dungeons and cells
Of a great dark jail.
Dreamed! rode pillion rather
With a demon in front of me
Upon a horse whose favourite hay
Was human hair.
Dream within dream dreamt I.
I dreamt a dream in which I woke
And, when awake, I killed a man.
Then, still in this dream, I fell asleep
And dreamt again that I woke
And pushed a woman over a cliff.
Next I choked a vivacious gentleman;
Then I stabbed a girl on an ottoman.
Each time the face of the man became
More like my father's face;
And that of the woman, of course,
Began to seem like my mother's.
As if I could have slain my parents
For that foul deed that struck
Me out of chaos, out of nothing.
At last I swam out of my nightmare
And managed to pray to Heaven
With its thousand white stars
To somehow stop my maddened mind
From making the reflection
Of reflection of my bad despair.
So then I dreamt my last dream.
I dreamt I was the bed
I slept upon and, lifeless, cared
Not what sack of blood and bones,
What pillar of dust
Made my springs creak
Or weighed me down.
At last I woke! (*Poems* 87)

The opening lines of 'Dream Within Dream' almost deliver a description of being entombed in the 'legal glass pyramid' of the 'Egypt' emblem. The difference is that 'Egypt' conveys a passive death state regarding the speaker's vision, whereas the speaker in 'Dream Within Dream' actively performs worse and worse deeds, feeling that he is awake, yet knowing that he is asleep. Like the Jonah face in a fish in 'Within Within', he is both active and acted upon. The nesting-box structure of the jail parallels the 'within within' structure of the dreams. The fact that the dreams are like a jail conveys that they are involuntary, inflicted upon the dreamer. Further, the jail suggests that the dreamer has been convicted of crime; the details of his offences appear a few lines later in the poem. The image of riding passenger on a horse with a demon in charge intensifies the speaker's panicked sense of being out of control, boxed in by forces much bigger than he. As the gender-specific murders that he commits metamorphose into matricide and patricide, we realize that the forces enclosing the speaker are psychological, self-generated — from within. So the within within nesting structure turns inside out, a form of demonic apocalypse. Clearly this poem takes place in the 'Fall' quadrant of the mythic cycle.

When the speaker manages to pray, and to swim out of his nightmare, he is still asleep, so obviously, even with the rebirth imagery, it is not a real awakening. He is still reflecting, as the man's eye in 'Within Within' is reflecting: leading away from particular things — in the case of 'Dream Within Dream', his body — and towards abstraction, the statement 'At last I woke!' We are left doubting that the dreamer has actually awakened; he may still be asleep. The point is that our fallen world is a state of sleep, and 'Dream Within Dream' ends there.

In regard to the poem's relationship to 'Within Within', besides the coincidence of images and concepts, 'Dream Within Dream' teaches us that the movement 'within within' does not necessarily tend towards revelation, but can be demonic. This difference clearly indicates that there is a moral dimension to the attainment of vision. 'Bad despair' leads to a horrible imprisonment within mirrors and dreams and runaway psychic urges. Imaginative creation and love, as 'Within Within' suggests, can lead to true vision.

The Tree

This emblem brings together two constellations of metaphors that are fundamental to Reaney's work, and that so far we have noted separately: Jungian alchemy and the philosophical insights of William Blake. The 'bringing together' here involves a process of displacement: substituting, in a given framework, something originally found in another context. In Jung's psychological theories, for instance, he displaces certain symbols and processes from alchemy, a physical, chemical domain, and uses them to define and label psychological, non-physical, entities. 'The Tree' displaces the Jungian individuation process, as the psychologist expresses it in alchemical terms, with Blake's biblically based cyclic myth, as interpreted by Frye. Structurally, the emblem further develops the systolic/diastolic 'within within' pattern, whereby 'within within' dynamically signals movement towards revelation as well as demonic movement away from it.

The picture in 'The Tree' features circles: circles within circles within circles. The centre-most of the ten concentric circles drawn in this illustration might remind us of the 'eye' diagram that Reaney mentions in 'Search for an Undiscovered Alphabet': 'the first letter in an alphabet of diagrams would have to be a simplification of the human eye — that is, a circle with a central dot' (39). With 'The Tree', we confront a complex eye indeed! In a small concession to imitative drawing, the outside circle, the thick wavy line, resembles bark on a cross-sectioned tree.

It is also critical to notice in the emblem's illustration that the circles are contained by a square that is formed from lines of various thicknesses. With this combination, and similarly to 'The Castle', the 'Tree' emblem leads us into the world of alchemical transformation. As we know, in the course of preparing his thesis on Spenser and Yeats, Reaney had studied C.G. Jung's book *Psychology and Alchemy*. Squaring the circle, the alchemical concept which the picture in 'The Tree' emblem sets forth, aims at the uniting of two opposites. J.E. Cirlot explains this 'equating of

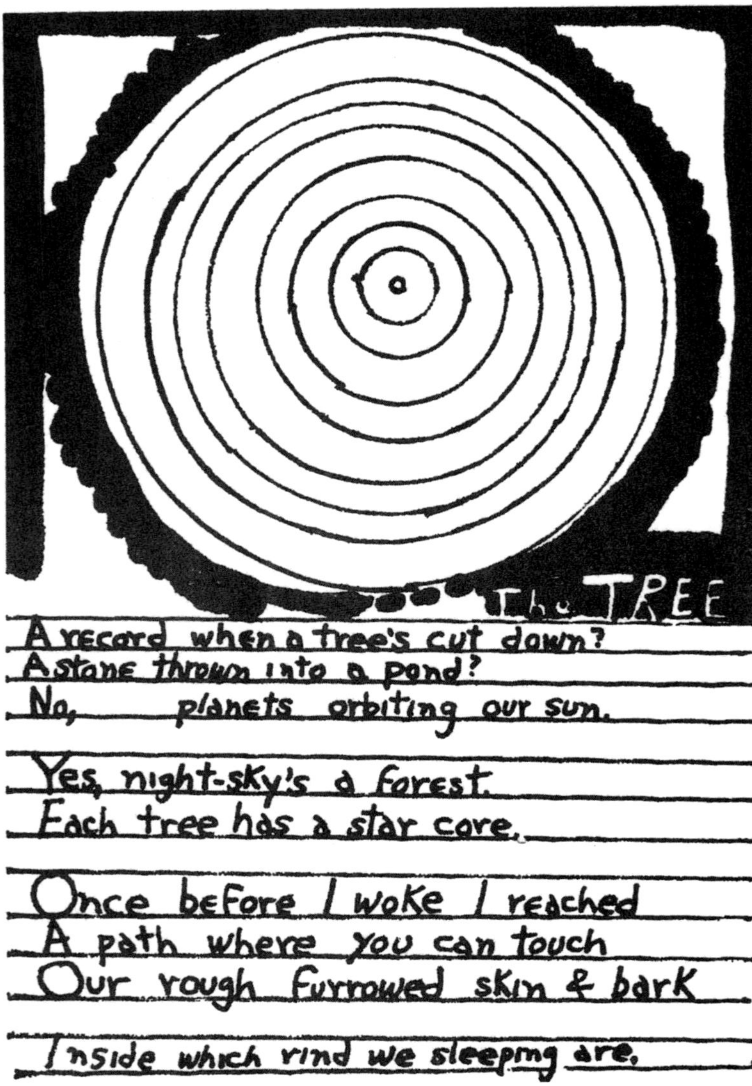
The TREE
A record when a tree's cut down?
A stone thrown into a pond?
No, planets orbiting our sun.
Yes, night-sky's a forest.
Each tree has a star core.
Once before I woke I reached
A path where you can touch
Our rough furrowed skin & bark
Inside which rind we sleeping are.

the two great cosmic symbols of heaven (or the circle) and earth (or the square)':

> The square was seen to correspond to the four Elements. The aim of 'squaring the circle', then (which strictly ought to be called 'circling the square'), was to obtain unity in the material world (as well as in the spiritual life) over and above the differences and obstacles (the static order) of the number four and the four-cornered square. (293)

Jung adapts — displaces — these alchemical ideas for his understanding of self-realization, as follows:

> the squaring of the circle is a stage on the way to the unconscious, a point of transit leading to a goal lying as yet unformulated beyond

'Squaring of the circle to make the two sexes one whole.' From Michael Maier. *Secretioris naturae secretorum scrutinium chymicum.* 1687, 221. Rpt. in Jung 122.

> it. It is one of those paths to the centre of the non-ego which were also trodden by the medieval investigators when producing the lapis [philosophers' stone]. (122)

From Jung's observations on squaring the circle we could infer that with 'The Tree' Reaney is creating an emblem to represent a moment in the individuation process. As we shall see, this process is itself transferred into a Blakean context.

The emblem's opening verbal dialogue formulates several interrogative interpretations by concentrating on different aspects of the picture. These questions and an answer create a back-and-forth, circumference/centre, series of pulsations:

• By focusing on the complete set of circles as a record — at once a vinyl album to be played on a phonograph, and a wooden cross-section — we imagine the way a phonograph's needle travels from circumference to centre, centripetally. The scientist's counting of annular rings might go in either direction, centripetally or centrifugally, but in numerical order, according to the tree's age, 1 would be at the centre, 10 at the circumference.

• By focusing on the centre, the place where a stone hits the water, the image creates centrifugal waves.

• By focusing on both the rings and the midpoint, we visualize planetary orbits encircling the central sun whose gravitational pull, like a magnet, keeps the planets in their circular courses.

The 'No' of the third line, a statement, not a question, seems to dismiss the record and stone theories in favour of the planetary orbits possibility. But the inward-outward pulse of the interpretations remains, and becomes in the fourth line the shift from day to night, a reversal of the previous sun image. Similarly, the single tree transforms to a forest, as the sun becomes one of multiple stars. Parallel to the process of squaring the circle, so the interplay of the picture and the metaphors in 'The Tree' imaginatively creates unity: the tree, which stands for the material world, uniting with the sun and stars, emblems of the sky and the spiritual world.

With the sixth line a change of voice — or in grammatical terms, 'person' — occurs, as the text shifts from the third person 'has' in line five, to the first person, initially the singular 'I', then the second person 'you' in line seven, and finally in lines eight and nine, the plurals 'Our' and 'we'. These changes in the subjects of the sentences again signal the process of unification. The word 'before' returns the text, however, to the world of time and space from which it had escaped through the metaphors of the text's opening sections. The repeated 'I' invokes individual points of view, establishing an awareness of personal disjunction. But quickly this separateness passes, through the word 'you', signifying both 'I' and 'we', and on to the coming together of 'Our' and 'we'.

The final two sections of the text are all one sentence. Since the single sentence is divided across two sections of the emblem's text, the reader is given to understand that the emblem's quest for unity has not been entirely successful. The text corroborates the momentariness of the unity in several ways. The path is 'reached'; that is, after a certain striving, the speaker arrives at the path, a state of awareness in which 'you can touch/Our rough furrowed skin & bark.' Now the metaphorical play has again inverted things: 'we' have metaphorically become the trees. And the outside circle of the emblem's picture has become 'our' enclosure, a metaphorical sleep. The haunting significance of the words which begin the text's closing sentence, 'Once before I woke', returns. As though we are multiply encircled, we exist in a dream world, the planet Earth, where glimpses of a path towards self-realization are possible and do take place, but at this stage 'we' are sleeping.

In connection with the work of squaring the circle, another observation which Jung makes about the uniting of opposites to reach the unconscious, relates directly to Reaney, and perhaps to how he was seeing himself in creating 'The Tree'. Jung quotes from a work entitled 'Instructio de arbore':

> 'I pray you, look with the eyes of the mind at the little tree of the grain of wheat, regarding all its circumstances, so that you may bring the tree of the philosophers to grow.' This seems to point to active imagination as the thing that sets the process really going. (243)

Like Blake, Jung concludes that the alchemical work is best done by artists. Blake's 'To see a World in a Grain of Sand' (431), of course, echoes in these words of Jung's, as does Blake's emphasis on imaginative energy. Frye explains the profound effects on Blake of John Milton's 1644 pamphlet *Areopagitica*, which argues against press censorship in a way that clarifies both Blake's understanding of the relation of religion to art, and of the role of the artist. *Areopagitica*, Frye writes,

> was undoubtedly a major influence in forming Blake's doctrine that the Christian Church cannot exist outside the arts because the secondary Word of God which unites us to the Primary Word or Person of Christ is a book and not a ceremony. (*Fearful Symmetry* 159)

Here Frye crystallizes an English Protestant theme, the word as the mediator between humanity and divinity, which is fundamental to the Reformation, and runs from Bunyan through Milton and Blake to Frye and to Reaney. Frye continues:

> The greatness of *Areopagitica* is that it speaks for liberty, not tolerance: it is not the plea of a nervous intellectual who hopes that a brutal majority will at least leave him alone, but a demand for the release of creative power and a vision of an imaginative culture in which the genius is not an intellectual so much as a prophet and seer. The release of creative genius is the only social problem that matters, for such a release is not the granting of extra privileges to a small class, but the unbinding of a Titan in man who will soon begin to tear down the sun and moon and enter Paradise. The creative impulse in man is God in man; the work of art, or the good book, is an image of God, and to kill it is to put out the perceiving eye of God. (*Fearful Symmetry* 159)

Frye's compelling words here, explaining *Areopagitica* through Blake's eyes, were no doubt intensely inspirational for Reaney. 'The Tree' demonstrates the emblem maker's ability to envision and share with his readers this democratic ideal. In 'The Tree', though, the ideal is just that: not yet realized. We are in the Redemption stage of the myth cycle. In the emblem's words, 'we sleeping are'.

Reaney's 1951 poem entitled 'In This Round Place' supplements and extends the imagery and themes of 'The Tree'. The 'round place' in the poem is 'This round blue head we live in'. So we dwell within a circular space in both the poem and the emblem, but there are key differences. With 'The Tree' the sense of enclosure applies to our entire bodies: the speaker comes close to breaking through 'Our rough furrowed skin & bark'; 'In This Round Place' focuses more closely on our heads, our minds, and in particular our rationality. The adjective 'blue' as applied to the 'head we live in' connotes sadness as well as the clear sky of thought. The poem develops by posing reasonable questions about various things, questions that are logically unanswerable. Reminiscent of the 'Egypt' emblem's preoccupation with perspective, 'In This Round Place' realizes that our situation amounts to trying to fit a square peg into a round hole, a demonic take on the squaring-the-circle theme: 'In this curved place He sent us to,/The curved mind cannot tell/Why the moon should fit the sun/In eclipses.' Untutored vision would equate the sizes of the sun and moon; astronomical science tells us different. 'What can the detective know for sure/In his hunt for the reason/Of a winter season/Or of whirlwinds and falling stars.' Not being ended with a question mark, this sentence is a statement about the inability of rationality to come to an understanding of such amazing yet ordinary events. The suggestion is that the faculty of reason is both inadequate and inappropriate for realizing our world. The poem then poses numerous questions that turn on comparisons: 'Why do the birds sing like silver hinges/to the doors of Heaven', for example. Such similes, again as we noted in the 'Egypt' emblem, compare distinct things, separating them, whereas metaphors identify and unite. So the effort to apply rationality to our world, 'In This Round Place' implies, is erroneous, a trap and dead end. Frye explains part of Blake's revulsion against the rationalist French philosopher Voltaire (the pen-name of François Marie Arouet, 1694–1778,) by citing his book *Micromégas,* that 'with its insistence on the immense distance and size of the stars, the miserable pettiness of man, and the blatant fatuity of the notion that this universe is anything with a human meaning, is instructively anti-Blakean' (*Fearful Symmetry* 378). 'In This Round Place' adopts this attitude which is opposed to such anti-human theories. Science's pitiful reduction of our human universe is epitomized in these lines:

The dust that hangs
In the air of a room
Teaches astronomers humble comparisons....

Scientists ignore the fact that perception is active, and instead of actively imagining things as they are, latch onto another thing that they consider comparable, for instance, the stars and planets: dust motes. Frye explains some consequences of this error by referring to Blake's analysis of Locke's form of reasoning:

> According to Locke ideas come from space into the mind; according to Blake space is a state of mind. But, as fallen man sees around him only the ruins of a fallen world which his own fall produced, space is a low state of mind. In higher states, where the world we live in is not objective but created, space is no longer an indefinite extent but the form of what we create. (*Fearful Symmetry* 48)

Blake's own words are striking in this regard:

> Error is Created; Truth is Eternal. Error, or Creation, will be Burned up, & then, & not till Then, Truth or Eternity will appear. It is burnt up the Moment Men cease to behold it. I assert for My Self that I do not behold the outward Creation & that to me it is hindrance & not Action; it is as the dirt upon my feet, No part of Me. 'What,' it will be Question'd, 'When the Sun rises, do you not see a round disk of fire somewhat like a Guinea?' O no, no, I see an Innumerable company of the Heavenly host crying, 'Holy, Holy, Holy is the Lord God Almighty.' I Question not my Corporeal or Vegetative Eye any more than I would Question a Window concerning a Sight. I look thro' it & not with it.

'The Tree' and 'In This Round Place' both dramatize the poet's awareness that although he intuits the dawn's existence as being a magnificent event of praise and thanksgiving, nevertheless he is stuck in the shrunken world of rational, divisive comparisons, and can see the sun only as a twenty-one-shilling coin. 'In This Round Place' metaphorically treats the fallen world in terms of a coffin, and goes on to present a 'within-within' type of image that parallels the emblematic eye-centred circles of 'The Tree':

> ... so certain
> Are we of the place where we're hid
> When of our coffin we have not discovered
> The doomsday to open the lid
> Nor have found yet
> That to open the eye is to shut an eye
> For in those opened seeing places
> Blindness and more closed eyelids lie.

The coffin's lid coalesces in this passage with the eye's, demonstrating the problem, as Blake says, with confusing the physical eye with the imagination, or in the poem's terms, failing to discover 'The doomsday to open the lid'. We persist in living in the fallen world, the world of ophthalmology not true apocalyptic vision, entombed inside the rings of the tree and our round blue heads.

The Red Heart includes two poems that resonate particularly with 'The Tree' and 'In This Round Place'. Even though coffins aren't usually circular, the poems' predominant metaphors, submarines and eggs, tend to round the body boxes' corners. Each poem is vividly imagined and, from the fallen point of view, macabre. The poems challenge readers to 'see beyond' gruesome details such as the 'wormy seas of earth' and the comparison of the Earth to a 'rotting head/That like a criminal's face/Severed and thrown from the block/Tumbles round and round....' But what is there to see as well? We are enabled to understand the infinite perspective that reveals death as the harbinger of new life. Death in both poems is the fallen state of death-in-life. The submarine-coffins' sailors are almost asleep, just dimly aware of their destination while being passively ferried in an underwater boat; the eggs laid by Queen Death in 'Coffins' offer the potential for real living. Together the two poems express the aspects of our death-in-life predicament that 'The Tree' also presents: the oblivious 'sleeping' state and the sense of potential awakening symbolized by the 'path' to 'touch/Our rough furrowed skin & bark'. More overtly than 'The Tree', these poems imagine the process

The Coffins

These coffins are submarines
That will sail beneath the slopes
Of grey-green old graveyards.

One white lone sailor to each
Submarine that navigates
The wormy seas of earth.

With shrouds for uniforms
Stitched by weeping tailors
These bony sailors
Shall sail deep field and morass
Without periscope or compass
They'll only dimly know
That someday they must flow
Into the final harbour
On some high grey shore
Where the Lord shall weigh
Men's wicked souls on Doomsday.

Coffins

Coffins are Death's eggs
Whose yolks, then, are the corpses
Of dead men and women,
Girls, boys and babies,
Girlfriends, boyfriends and lovers,
Death lays them in her cool nest
That is the gravelly ancient breast
Of Earth, that rotting head
That like a criminal's face
Severed and thrown from the block
Tumbles round and round
The pitying merciful Sun.

And Death, her children laid
(With Abel as her nest-egg),
Then waits for them to hatch
Upon the branches of a dead tree
Which neither wind nor rain
Can strike down or revive.
She waits, oh centuries! in vain
For never will the pharaoh hid
In secret room within the pyramid
Rise for her from his golden bed
Until Queen Death herself is dead.

of rebirth, in the case of 'The Coffins', as a 'final harbour', and in the case of 'Coffins', as eggs hatching. The second verse of 'Coffins' has in it two items familiar to us from the emblems: a tree and a pyramid. Both are at once sites of captivity as well as sites of possible liberation. Circling back to 'The Tree', we are ready now to consider how such oxymorons, the juxtaposing of contraries, function in the emblem.

In the fourth issue of Reaney's journal *Alphabet* he addresses the contraries 'universal' and 'local'. His tree metaphor in the passage magnetically brings to mind 'The Tree'. Reaney's way of thinking about the 'local'/'universal' or 'native'/'international' conundrum is also instructive, in that it parallels his approach in the emblem. He starts with questions that he has been asked:

> 'What do we need a native drama for?' 'Why all this absurd nationalism?' I don't believe you can really be world or unprovincial or whatever until you've sunk your claws into a very locally coloured tree trunk and scratched your way through to universality. (3)

The gist is that we need to comprehend both, not just one, of the various contraries that Reaney mentions. With 'The Tree' we have already noted the alchemical/psychological process of squaring the circle, an image of uniting opposites. The circular illustration and text of 'The Tree' are also contraries, the text being laid out within ruled straight lines. And the concentric circles, whose diagrammatic character is an eye, simultaneously illustrate a 'systolic/diastolic' movement: both plunging within within, towards the central vision, and the opposite, where 'within within' means being directed towards and inside the beholder. Or to put this dynamic another way: the beholder is both at the centre and at the circumference of the drawing.

To explain the importance of this vision, which 'The Tree' and the poems magnetically arranged by it permit us, once again Frye's explanation in *Fearful Symmetry* of Blake's thought is helpful. In Blake's distinction between 'Selfhood', natural, fallen humanity, and unfallen 'Man', he first defines the state of sleep or death-in-life that figures in all of the works we have considered. Frye expounds: 'We are born into a fallen world and are therefore born with a 'natural' tendency to make the most rather than the best of it, to accept it as final reality' (*Fearful Symmetry* 58). He goes on to say that this 'state of nature' is 'that state of animal self-absorption which Blake calls the Selfhood' (*Fearful Symmetry* 58). However, Frye writes,

> Man has within him the principle of life and the principle of death: one is the imagination, the other the natural man. In the natural world the natural principle will win out eventually and the man will die....
>
> The only possible cure for the original sin of this Selfhood of the natural man is vision, the revelation that this world is fallen and therefore not ultimate. (*Fearful Symmetry* 58)

'The Tree' and the poems 'Inside this Round Place', 'The Coffins', and 'Coffins', taken together in the magnetic force field that the emblem sets up, reveal precisely this last point, 'that this world is fallen and therefore not ultimate'.

A one man band? Understand
& you can
This is a Man

THE RIDDLE

The Riddle

'The Riddle' is the first emblem of chapter two of the emblem book; as does 'The Castle', the first emblem of chapter one, 'The Riddle' contains a symbolic image of 'Man'. The emblems do not mirror each other, but they do bear key similarities. The top shape in both is a circle, but the other two components of the illustrations are markedly different. Instead of the cross-hatched rectangle and the semi-circle-studded inverted triangle in 'The Castle', in 'The Riddle' a heart and a spiral appear. At the base of the illustrations are the textual components, which in these two emblems set up dialogues with their respective graphic elements. Seen in another light, the textual features could be considered as components — the verbal faculty — of human beings. The texts of the two emblems both close with the '-an' rhyme, and in relation to the respective images, the texts function similarly, as somewhat cryptic explanations of the emblems' texts. However, 'The Riddle' offers its challenge to 'Understand' more overtly than 'The Castle', explicitly directing the viewer to parse the symbolic cluster.

The emblem's title, 'The Riddle', in combination with its solution, might remind readers of the myth of the Sphinx, the strangler who challenged ill-fated Oedipus on his way to Thebes in Boeotia. This Grecian sphinx, derived mythologically from the Egyptian sphinx, combined the body of a lion with eagle's wings and a woman's head. Such a combination of body parts from three different sources, an animal's, a bird's and a human being's, parallels Reaney's tripartite emblematic drawing. Like a musical 'band', the human being's distinct parts contribute their unique roles to making a whole, so the answer to the emblem's first question is 'yes'.

The riddle which the Sphinx posed to Oedipus, the 'banned' prince, and to all travellers on the way to Thebes, highlights numbers to express its theme: 'What is it that has one voice, is four-footed first, two-footed second, then three-footed?' Avoiding death by strangulation for a wrong solution to the riddle, Oedipus correctly answered, 'a man': an infant crawls on all fours, grows up to walk on two feet, and in old age adds a staff to the two feet. Having had to use the head to reach this solution, and regarding the circular drawing in the way we explained this shape in 'The Castle', we move on to consider the heart shape.

In preparation for burial, the ancient Egyptians left only one internal organ in mummies, the heart. They regarded it as essential to the body's continued life in eternity. Along with the brain and the sexual organs, the heart has always been regarded as one of the focal points of human being. Reaney's illustration has the heart at the centre of the figure. The heart began to be challenged as the seat of human intelligence, wisdom, love, and even soul when Western anatomical science developed, starting with René Descartes's description of the human body as a mechanism and the heart as a hydraulic pump. Through their hearts, people believed, the deity communicated directly: heart to heart. In the eighteenth century, to promote and celebrate such communication, and to supply a more passionate alternative to Descartes's technical model, the Roman Catholic Church established the Cult of the Sacred Heart, with Christ's heart as the symbol of incarnation and loving sacrifice on behalf of his people.[1] Much as we say the sun rises even though scientists teach us that this apparent rising is on account of the Earth's rotating, we still speak about the heart as central to our beings, although psychologists tell us otherwise: 'cross my heart', we promise; 'take it to heart', we advise; 'broken heart', we moan; 'wholeheartedly', we cheer.

Reaney's conventional drawing of a heart is located in the centre of the emblem's symbolic body. He had first presented a drawing similar to the illustration of 'The Riddle' in his 1965 'Search for an Undiscovered Alphabet' article in *Canadian Art*, titling it 'my diagram of a man — mind, ♥ and belly' (38). The depth of Reaney's thought as a symbolist shows through in his spontaneous use of the ♥ in place of the word 'heart'. He also made an emblem with a similar illustration, but with different text. It was not published, however.

Jung refers to a charming myth that relates the heart to the gold of alchemy, and demonstrates the sort of symbolic thinking that Reaney's emblems require of us:

> The sun, by its many millions of revolutions, spins the gold into the

earth. Little by little the sun has imprinted its image on the earth, and that image is the gold. The sun is the image of God, the heart is the sun's image in man, just as gold is the sun's image in the earth (also called *Deus terrenus*), and God is known in the gold. (330)

Below the head and heart is a spiral, in the position of the third of the body's energy centres. The 'belly', as Reaney calls it, includes the reproductive organs. As with 'The Castle', we have a female symbol composing what is called in this emblem too, 'Man'. Cirlot describes the spiral as 'A schematic image of the evolution of the universe' (290). He also notes the belief that spirals 'may be regarded as figures intended to induce a state of ecstasy and to enable man to escape from the material world and to enter the beyond, through the "hole" symbolized by the mystic centre' (292). Psychologically, the spiral itself represents for Jung the process of individuation, of circling the unreachable centre. 'Often one has the impression that the personal psyche is running round this central point like a shy animal,' Jung writes, 'at once fascinated and frightened, always in flight, and yet steadily drawing nearer' (208). Reaney's emblem, with its Oedipal and Jungian elements, certainly supports interpretations pointing to human spiritual development.

Somewhat related to these interpretations of the spiral is that of William Butler Yeats, on whose work Reaney wrote his doctoral thesis. People familiar with Yeats know that the spiral was a major symbolic shape for the Irish poet, and that he calls spirals 'gyres' and 'cones'. They indicate the shape of human beings' trajectories through various spiritual stages of life and death. The complex esoteric patterns that Yeats worked out are based on teachings of groups such as the Freemasons and the Order of the Golden Dawn; Reaney's thesis explores the intricacies of Yeats's esoteric system largely in order to demonstrate its relationship with the more straightforward classical and biblical foundations of Spenser's writings, as well as those of Percy Bysshe Shelley (1792–1822) and William Blake, who are also part of this 'mythopoeic' tradition to which, Reaney argues, Yeats also belongs. To show Reaney's assessment of Yeats's work, it is most useful to quote from the conclusion to 'The Influence of Spenser on Yeats':

> We have shown that Yeats has links with Spenser. As a natural outgrowth of this discovery we found that the reason some of these links seem so strong is because Yeats and Spenser take their place in something larger than themselves, the particular tradition already mentioned.... When we connect Yeats with Spenser and with the winged horse which all the members of the mythopoeic tradition believe in, we are helping to make Yeats more popular, less 'strange and obscure, and unreal'. Having once attended a disastrous public lecture on Yeats where the speaker illustrated the gyres of Yeats' system with corkscrews and spit curls made out of paper to everyone's total lack of enlightenment I think that the approach to Yeats made through an accepted poet who has no bizarre system up his sleeve probably helps one to accept Yeats also as a poet working in a perfectly acceptable and hoary tradition. The more one sees that Yeats' poetry goes back to the Renaissance and not to late nineteenth century table-rappings the more delightful is the reading of it. (257–58)

In this conclusion to his thesis Reaney offers his sense of the limits of symbolism. As an active participant in the mythopoeic tradition himself, he respected these limits. So although it might be tempting to delve into the hermetic mysteries, in this study we too have avoided and will continue to avoid such esoteric investigations because they are fundamentally irrelevant to Reaney's art.[2]

Until now, this book primarily has taken a thematic approach to Reaney's emblems and the other works that they magnetically form into patterns. With 'The Riddle' the emblems' style will be brought more prominently into the discussion. Rather than exaggeratedly separating form from content, though, the aim here is to gain insight into Reaney's artistic techniques in the emblems' illustrations in order to supplement our understanding of their effects. In a sense, we are responding to Reaney's wondering, in 'Search for an Undiscovered Alphabet',

> what if one were to look directly at diagrams instead of looking at them through words or music or photography. Is there a possible key to the way they can directly express reality? (38–39)

Since Reaney's pictures in his emblems are diagrammatic, not realistic drawings, their simplicity opens possibilities for profound symbolism, as we have seen to some extent already. Reaney's thinking in metaphors drawn from the domain of alchemy, a body of knowledge that he learned in good measure from C.G. Jung's *Psychology and Alchemy*, was probably stimulated by Northrop Frye's use in his literary theory of the psychologist's concept of archetypes. In Jung's writings, an archetype is an inherited primitive mental image which exists in the collective unconscious; for Frye, an archetype is 'a typical or recurring image.... [,] a symbol which connects one poem with another and thereby helps to unify and integrate our literary experience' (*Anatomy* 99). By applying and extending these definitions, it is evident, Reaney developed in his emblems a grammar of simple shapes that hold worlds of potential meanings.

Rhoda Kellogg's work, in *The Psychology of Children's Art* and *Analyzing Children's Art*, was a 'big influence'[3] on the style of the illustrations in Reaney's emblems. Kellogg regards children's art as the 'groundwork of all art' (*Psychology* 95). Although Kellogg writes that her detailed study of children's art 'is not based on Jungian psychology' (*Analyzing* 68), both Jung and Kellogg place great emphasis on the significance and universality of simple shapes such as the circle, mandala (the Sanskrit word for disc), rectangle and triangle. Kellogg discovered in conversation with Jung in 1954 that they do agree that children's art is archetypal, but they explain this quality differently. For Jung, the archetypes are inborn images which manifest themselves through the mediation of symbols. For Kellogg, every child's art develops through scribbles into basic shapes. In other words, as an observer of children's art-making behaviour, Kellogg found in it the same sort of universality as that which Jung hypothesized as originating in the psyche. Referring specifically to the mandala, a shape that all children draw, Kellogg writes:

> If all individuals have similar experiences with the Mandala, then it may be rightly called an image of the collective unconscious. In the same way all the basic forms of art may be called archetypal. (*Analyzing* 231)

Reaney does use simple, universal shapes in his emblems, as do such abstract artists as Mondrian, Picasso, Chagall, Klee, Kandinsky and Riopelle. They do so in order to manipulate profoundly communicative, universally recognized, human symbols. And, again to connect Reaney's Modernist abstract art work with the earlier Protestant English emblem tradition, it is noteworthy that in his study of Renaissance English emblematists Roger Sharrock deemed the basis of their strategies for symbolizing to be the 'desire to find meaning in the most ordinary things' (106). In Reaney's emblems, these 'things' are elemental shapes.

Kellogg emphasizes the universal quality of children's art. Based on her extensive observations, she writes that

> Cultures the world over, however simple or advanced, use the same forms to express what they wish to say....
>
> The art of young children everywhere is identical. It comes from the same beginnings and uses the same shapes found in primitive art. The walls of tombs and the shards of ancient pottery and the finger paintings of today's child each bear the same testimony — that in art all mankind is one. (*Psychology* 105)

The Modernist quest for universally recognized and available symbols was also being carried on by nearby associates of Reaney's. A prime example is William Ronald, born in Stratford in the same year as Reaney, 1926. To promote abstract art in Canada, in 1953 Ronald founded Painters Eleven, a loosely-knit group that included Harold Town, Jack Bush and other influential painters and sculptors. It is clear from Ronald's painting that his work is based on child-like drawing combined with sophisticated symbolism. In his sun shapes and dashed square borders we find the kind of squaring-the-circle image that is familiar to us from Reaney's emblem 'The Tree'.

Another influential principle of Kellogg's is that 'children's work is just as artistically pleasing as the work of adults' (*Analyzing* 43). In fact, it may be more so, she implies:

> Adult art differs from child art in those art styles and formulas that are taught to older children in each culture and that help to distinguish one culture from another. In some cultures, the special styles and formulas require considerable technique. When technique departs too far from basic esthetic forms, however, it seems to lose vitality, as the history of academic painting clearly suggests. (*Analyzing* 43)

From these words of Kellogg's, and from his understanding of the constricting effects of perspective, as we saw in the 'Egypt' emblem, Reaney might well have felt the impetus towards using basic simple forms in his emblems.

A third principle asserted by Kellogg, based on her extensive observations of children's artwork, is that children's art develops out of itself. This principle is similar to Frye's theory of literature's being made from other literature. Kellogg defines twenty basic scribbles which children make progressively, and says that they are 'the building blocks of art' (*Analyzing* 14). Once children get to the stage of combining line formations, adults tend to apply labels to their work. Kellogg, however, maintains that, for example,

> the Humans [that children draw] are not drawn from life, nor are they crude, immature, stumbling efforts in art. They represent an advanced stage of the child's evolving mental capacity to create complex Gestalts of great interest to the human eye. (*Analyzing* 108)

From simple scribbles and shapes, children move towards overall patterns and therefore concepts. In the literary context, Frye calls this process attaining a 'synoptic view' (*Anatomy* 3). The simplicity of style apparent in Reaney's emblems may be explained by a similar desire on his part — a desire to discover fundamental human patterns in the chaos of life, a desire which is not, after all, childish.

Instantly, the 'Riddle' emblem draws into its force field three of Reaney's paintings, which were displayed side by side at the 2008 McMichael Gallery exhibition of Reaney's art work. The magnetic patterns take shape from the subjects of the four works, but mainly from the stylistic topics that 'The Riddle' raises, and that we have been considering in the light of Reaney's article 'Search for an Undiscovered Alphabet' as well as Kellogg's studies of children's art.[4] In form, the three paintings themselves constitute riddles; they are each multidimensional 'within within' configurations of symbols, allusions and quotations. Since the dating of the paintings is only tentative, it is preferable not to interpret them as a sequence, but rather as a trio of interrelated works that both as a group and individually illuminate and are illuminated by 'The Riddle'. Thematically the paintings combine autobiographical details with universal patterns, as Reaney considered them, patterns that he intuited, and later learned systematically from the writings of Spenser, Blake, Yeats, Jung and Frye.

Foremost, and excitingly for students of Reaney's emblems, in 'Pen' the red-haired figure holds the illustration for the 'Riddle' emblem, and the figure in 'Frond' holds the illustration for 'The Castle'. The figure in 'Brush' holds a rectangular object with three coloured circles. Here we have an opportunity, as Reaney suggests in the 'Undiscovered Alphabet' article, 'to look directly at diagrams instead of looking at them through words or music or photography' (39). The non-verbal, diagrammatic logic of the three illustrations, two quoted from emblems, is as follows: the illustration in 'Brush', showing three coloured circles, resembles the other two illustrations in the use of the circle shape and in there being three parts to each illustration, so with wit — a limited amount of it, let's admit — we connect the three. The triple circles, however, are not purely emblematic, since on another level and in the context of the painting, they represent a watercolourist's palette that consists of the primary

The Artist & Table (c. 1991) — 'Brush'

The Painter's Table (c. 1994) — 'Pen'

The Poet's Table #2 (c. 1992) — 'Frond'

colours, yellow, red, blue. Enlarging this pattern of thought, we return to the other two illustrations, and transfer the notion of a palette to the circle, heart, spiral of 'Pen', and to the circle, rectangle, triangle of 'Frond'; the symbolic dimensions of these shapes, as we have explored them, function in 'Pen' and 'Frond' as the raw materials with which the paintings' figures make art.

We could go on from this transference to note that the middle terms of each illustration, 'Brush': circle; 'Pen': heart; 'Frond': rectangle, are all red in colour, and thereby we generate a fourth and different illustration: red circle, red heart, red rectangle. Now all we have to do is come up with an appropriate text, and we'd be in the emblem-making business ourselves. That may sound facetious, but it is precisely the aim of Reaney's art: to involve his audience so that their perceptions are active and imaginative. In person and in his works, Reaney often approvingly referred to the maxim that William Blake formulated in 1799, writing to his patron Dr Trusler:

> The wisest of the Ancients consider'd what is not too Explicit as the fittest for Instruction, because it rouzes the faculties to act.

To those less attuned to Reaney's emblems than we are, there could be even more obvious connections among the works than the emblem illustrations, such as the similar human figures in the paintings. At a glance the artist, painter and poet, all seated in similar postures on chairs at tables, share numerous family resemblances: similarly shaped heads, hairlines, noses, eyes, ears, mouths, torsos, hands. Each wears a shirt of a different cloth cut from the same pattern. And each sports a butterfly perched on his nose. The butterflies, like the shirts, are all differently coloured, though. The rooms in the background are also different. The artist has a black complexion, the painter white, the poet brownish red. Are they racially different? Or perhaps the colourations symbolize varying moods. As this possibility is expressed, it becomes plain that in order to realize the meanings of these paintings, we have to adjust our reading of the images away from noticing similar and dissimilar physical details to actively perceiving and working out the paintings' numerous symbolic energies.

First, let's recognize the elephant in the room: these are in no sense of the word 'realistic' paintings of people. They could be more accurately called cartoons than portraits. As such, the figures themselves are as thoroughly symbolic as are their colourations. Two of the paintings, 'Pen' and 'Frond,' non-verbally come right out and remind us that we are working with symbols. Both paintings incorporate miniature sketches of the larger coloured cartoon figures: top right corner of 'Pen,' and top right corner of the table in 'Frond'. The butterflies too, though they might cause us a sympathetic tickle on the nose, are symbolic: with their life cycle from egg to larva to cocoon to winged adult, they stand for the metamorphosis that art brings about, the transmutation of the chaotic fallen world into words and pictures, music, dance, and other visions of eternity, as Blake might put it. The illustration on the frontispiece of Blake's emblem book *For the Sexes: The Gates of Paradise* shows a caterpillar overlooking a human-faced butterfly cocoon; the emblem's riddling title, which might have inspired Reaney's answering emblem, 'The Riddle', is 'What is Man?' (Keynes 760). The McMichael exhibition of Reaney's artwork quoted a note of Richard Stingle's in which he says that the butterfly indicates 'the triumph of life over death'.

Complementary to the symbolic butterflies are the various artworks displayed on the three tables. They represent the artefacts themselves, as distinct from the process and implications of creating them, as the butterflies do. In the same way that the circle-heart-spiral of 'Pen' recalls the illustration of 'The Riddle', and the circle-rectangle-triangle of 'Frond' recalls the illustration of 'The Castle', some of the artworks within the paintings invoke artworks that Reaney had already created either as stand-alone paintings or in other contexts. In 'Brush' the three items on the table represent, from left to right, 'Rural Dandy', an early sketch that exists in various versions and settings[5]; the killdeer from Reaney's 'Emblem for the township of my birth';[6] and 'Cyclist'.[7] In the 'Brush' painting, these versions of earlier uncoloured drawings have become completed paintings. In 'Pen', however, the art on the table is a collection of pen-and-ink sketches. There is another version of the 'Cyclist' (bottom middle), and a revision of a decorative sketch (bottom right) that appeared in *Twelve Letters to a Small Town* (*Poems* 214), just before the Third Letter, titled 'Orange Lilies'. Whereas in the *Twelve Letters* context the chicken is running with a castle on her back, in 'Pen' she carries a house. The prone woman (top right) who seems to be in the process of being sketched, connects with the woman in 'Frond'.

In an upcoming chapter on 'The Last House' we will delve further into Reaney's use of quotations. For now it is enough to note that part of Reaney's motivation in his artistic productions, as he told Jean McKay in an interview in 2006, was his desire to 'keep a record' of his explorations. To that extent, the intertextuality — the quotations and allusions to other works — in the three 'Table' paintings could be interpreted as autobiographical details, and therefore the three artist figures would be phases of James Reaney at work. But this explanation of the paintings needs to be supplemented. The inclusion of 'The Riddle' and 'The Castle' in the field of meaning, as we are doing, and as the paintings themselves do, directs us to broaden our interpretation from the autobiographical to the universal. In this time of Postmodernism, we have to remember that along with most other Modernist thinkers and artists, Reaney believed in universality; Kellogg, Jung, Frye, and Reaney in particular, thought that human life everywhere is organized in the cyclical pattern of birth, fall, redemption, apocalypse. 'The Riddle' proposes that its diagram 'is a Man'; 'The Castle' illustration 'is the ground plan/For a castle called Man'. In the same way, the three 'Table' paintings make more general statements. Autobiographical elements are just that: parts of a more inclusive field of relations. This approach is corroborated by the cartoon style of the artist figures. A more general thematic statement could be that the paintings illustrate the understanding, common to Blake, Frye and Reaney, that the artist, like an alchemist, transmutes life's unruliness into the eternal forms of art. We can see, then, that for Reaney simplification is not only a technique for accomplishing this transformation of life to poetic and visual art, but also a symbol of the transformation process itself: life and art are clearly not the same.

Three of the outline sketches on the table in 'Frond', the man with his hat, praying to a rock or egg; the child with a circular mouth and head with sun-like rays for hair; and the woman with her circular head and breasts, taken together, point to themes of family, the coincidence of male and female in the child, and perhaps the centrality of the child in human life. The child, of course, is freshest from (re-)birth, so is an epiphany or revelation of the possibility for renewal in human life. The child state in all of us is when we recognize and act upon this consciousness, as discoverers and communicators of it. Thus the three 'Table' paintings ignore the laws of perspective that have to be taught to children. Instead of restricting the viewers' eyes to one solitary point of view, where the vanishing point would decree, Reaney's paintings present viewers with configurations of equally central features. For example, the little sketch in the table's upper right-hand corner, as mentioned, is a parenthetical reminder of the artifice involved with 'Frond' as a whole.

The words 'The Undergrad' beneath that small sketch allude to the University College student magazine of that name, to which Reaney contributed poems and drawings extensively from 1945 to 1948, while he was an undergraduate at the University of Toronto. As an autobiographical detail, the mention of 'The Undergrad', along with the mini-sketch of the artist figure in 'Frond', read in proper perspective, indicates how important the publication was to Reaney's development as a poet and visual artist. In particular, it was at this time that *The Undergrad* published his story 'The Box Social'; it created a Canada-wide uproar. Reaney calls this episode 'one of the key turning points of my college career, even more crucial than the publication of my first book of poems.' He realized then that Southwestern Ontario was as good a place as any to be a setting for Gothic fiction and drama, what he called 'neo-Gothic' ('James Crerar Reaney' 303–4). The neo-Gothic strain in Reaney's work occurs often, and culminates with his *Donnellys* trilogy of plays, which corroborate a significant observation by Blake in regard to historians. Blake gives to readers and viewers of paintings on historical subjects

> the historical fact in its poetical vigour so as it always happens, and not in that dull way that some Historians pretend, who, being weakly organized themselves. Cannot see either miracle or prodigy; all is to them a dull round of probabilities and possibilities; but the history of all times and places is nothing else but improbabilities and impossibilities; what we should say was impossible if we did not see it always before our eyes. (*Blake: Complete* 578.)

Autobiographically, then, the small sketch and the words 'The Undergrad' are portentous. As part of the universal themes also in play in the 'Riddle' emblem, 'The Undergrad' stands for a breakthrough, an occasion when private life experiences became public art. In a painting employing conventional perspective, it is hard to say where such a tiny fragment with such big implications would appear, if at all.

The fern frond that the artist in 'Frond' is using to draw the background of the child sketch might be an allusion to the line in the 'Within Within' emblem, 'This crystal holds a mineral fern.' As we noted in connection with that emblem, the mineral fern in the crystal is the human pattern created by perception. So the use of the fern in 'Frond' extends the sense of perception — an action, we remember — to the act of drawing and creativity more generally.

And once again, the 'Riddle' emblem directs our attention to the style of the drawings displayed on the tables in the three paintings. 'The Riddle' illustration is diagrammatic, to be sure, and laden with symbolic suggestions. It also brings to mind another important principle of Blake's that informs all of Reaney's emblems, and is elaborated further by the 'Table' paintings. In connection with the 'Within Within' emblem, we noted in Frye's description of culture's central myth that the cyclical states of birth, fall, redemption, apocalypse revolve around four major antitheses. (See page 94.) In Art, the antithesis is outline versus imitation. Blake's expression of his preference is characteristically vigorous, not to say feisty.

> The great and golden rule of art, as well as of life, is this: That the more distinct, sharp and wirey the bounding line, the more perfect the work of art, and the less keen and sharp, the greater is the evidence of weak imitation, plagiarism and bungling.... What is it that builds a house and plants a garden, but the definite and determinate.... Leave out this line, and you leave out life itself; all is chaos again, and the line of the almighty must be drawn out upon it before man or beast can exist. (*Blake: Complete* 585; qtd. in *Fearful Symmetry* 97.)

As with the 'Riddle' emblem's illustration, so also the 'Table' paintings: the 'bounding line' is unmistakeable throughout. Although perhaps more obviously so in the drawings and paintings that are exhibited on the tables, the same firmness of line is certainly shown in the paintings as whole configurations.

'The Riddle' asks, 'A one man band?' We have already suggested that the answer is 'Yes', and that the three centres of energy — mind, heart and belly — each come into play in creating the music that is our lives. With this music in our ears, then, from the spiral 'belly' shape in 'The Riddle', we leap to the spiralling, singing 'Windlady'.

---

1. For a recent account of the origins and influence of the Cult of the Sacred Heart, see Jonas.

2. Readers who cannot resist could find a place to begin at http://www.orderofthe-goldendawn.org/.

3. Reaney stated this during our telephone conversation of 15 May 2001. He also mentions Kellogg's psychology specifically in 'Vision in Canada?' (945).

4. The titles and dates of these paintings as they appear here are those used for the McMichael Gallery's exhibition, The Iconography of the Imagination: The Art of James Reaney. January 26 to May 18, 2008. See http://www.mcmichael.com/exhibitions/jamesreaney/indexpast.cfm. The titles used in the exhibition for 'The Artist & Table' and 'The Painter's Table' seem to be reversed, since in the former the figure holds a paintbrush, while the figure in the latter holds a dip pen and displays pen-and-ink sketches, not paintings. Therefore, for the sake of clarity, I will refer to the paintings by the implement held by each figure: 'Brush', 'Pen', 'Frond'.

5. See, for example, *Performance Poems* (24), and McMichael exhibition item L2007.7.50. In the *Windsor Review* interview, Reaney calls this sketch a 'self-portrait' (15). It is also used in his Ad for Remainders (see p 181).

6. See, for example, *Performance Poems* (37).

7. See, for example, McMichael exhibition item L2007.7.54, where on the sketch was handwritten the following note/poem: 'That's me on the Old Road turning/Down into our long farm lane./I loved my bicycle and often/Rode over to McCallum's farm/To practise piano duets.'

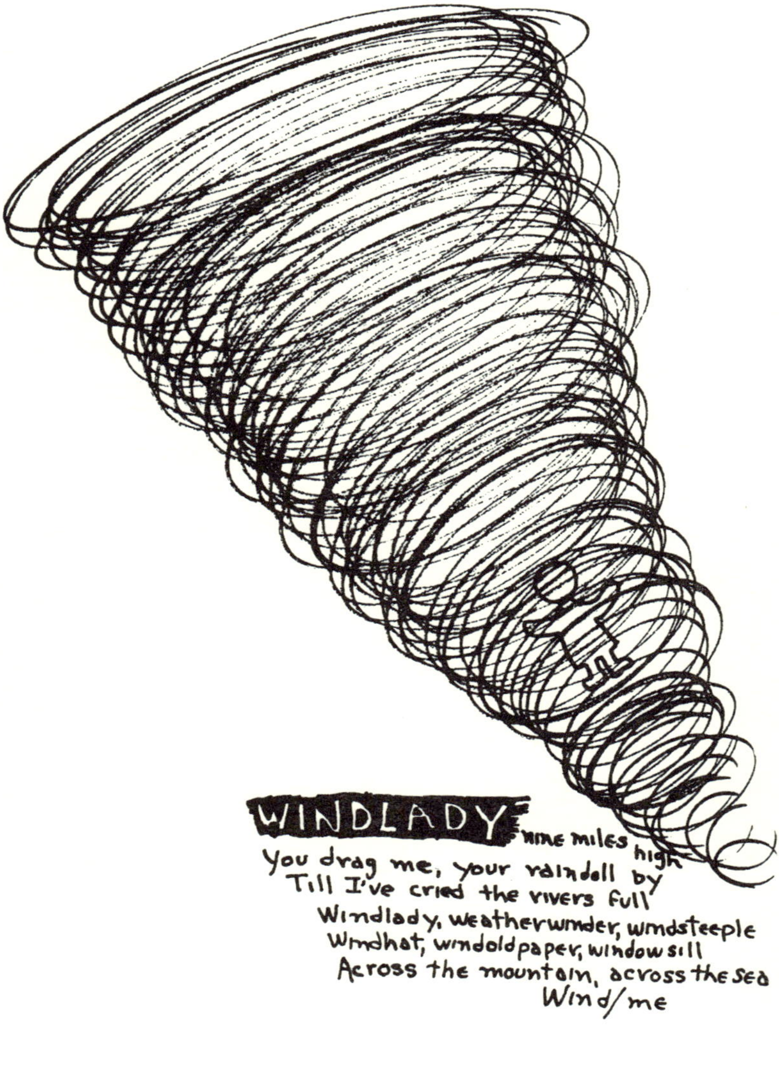
WINDLADY nine miles high
You drag me, your raindoll by
Till I've cried the rivers full
Windlady, weatherwinder, windsteeple
Windhat, windoldpaper, windowsill
Across the mountain, across the sea
Wind/me

Windlady

The diagrammatic quality of the illustrations of Reaney's emblems is present in 'Windlady', but less markedly so than with the simple spiral shape in 'The Riddle'. In 'Windlady' there is also a hint of pictorial realism: the visual image does suggest a tornado funnel, a 'windlady', with a little 'rain doll' inside it. Drawn from the side, the spiral, one of all children's basic scribbles, as Kellogg demonstrates, is a whirlwind (*Analyzing* 21). As a traditional symbolic form the spiral is a shape which induces ecstasy — literally, standing outside oneself — and thereby offers a path to another world, an experience of transcendence (Cirlot 291). As an instrument in the 'one man band' that is 'Man' in 'The Riddle', the text of 'Windlady' gives voice to the pictured cut-out rain doll riding the cyclone.

Rain dolls are used ritually to bring on rain in many parts of the world, particularly Japan, Brazil, Cuba, the United States, and also in Zulu and some West African cultures, the last of which include the sources of Haitian Voodoo. Rather than referring to specific Voodoo rituals, however, as does 'Baron Samedi Porte Baton', the emblem to be explored in the next chapter, Reaney's 'Windlady' emblem is evidence of this Southwestern Ontario artist's effort to generate a symbol that draws on the mythopoeic tradition and yet is appropriate to his own place and culture.

The rain doll in 'Windlady' voices this generative dimension; her act of speaking symbolizes artistic creation, including linguistic creation. The word 'Windlady' is Reaney's neologism, perhaps based on 'windlass'. [A powerful machine for winding, winching, and hauling, powers that a tornado also has. This forcefulness is part of the windlady too.] He also could have had in mind a 1925 poem 'The Wind Is A Lady With', by e.e. cummings, a poet famous for his own neologisms. As in 'Windlady', the speaker in the cummings poem addresses the wind. As well, the wind itself is a 'green person' who regenerates the land, and 'wanders/imminently across the renewed world'. In 'Windlady' the rain doll humanizes the tornado, feminizes it, and emphasizes not what we might expect, the wind's destructiveness, but rather its creative powers, powers we have observed already in connection with the spiral symbol. As the rain doll's ritual presence generates rain in a dry season, her voice gives birth to new words: 'Windlady, weatherwinder, windsteeple/Windhat, windoldpaper', coming to rest on 'windowsill'. This creative process, emblematized by the wordplay's making insights and connections, transforms the rain doll, identifying her with the vortex of moving air: 'Wind/me.'

'Windlady' magnetically attracts two in particular of Reaney's other works: the 1956 poem 'Windyard', and the play *Listen to the Wind,* first performed in 1966.

The Windyard

I built a windyard for the wind;
    The wind like a wild vast dog came up
To play with weathervanes and corners
    My keyholes and my chinks.

And for the sea I built a well;
    The brookish tomcat gurgled in,
Waterfell and sprung about
    Hunting throats and boots.

I stood a house up from the earth;
    The mappy girl came in
With rut and footstep path
    That wind the traveller up.

A stove I hammered for the sun;
    In flew the golden oriole
To crackle sticks of time
    And sing the loaves of space.

Come girl well yard and stove,

> Come Flesh Heart Mind and Lyre,
> Come Earth Water Wind and Fire.
> Well, when they came
> Barking, meowing, talking and carolling,
> I stepped above both house and yard
> Into myself.

The term 'windyard' is, like 'windlady', a neologism, a word newly generated in the poem. The emblem 'Windlady' relates the three elements of air, water and earth. The wind lifts the rain doll so that she 'cried the rivers full', then sweeps 'Across the mountain, across the sea'. These sequential images yield an exciting regenerative energy that might actually be the text's unnamed fire. The poem 'Windyard' explicitly includes air, water, earth and fire, the classical four elements that underlie the signs of astrology. Perhaps the most striking thematic similarity between the text of 'Windlady' and the poem 'Windyard' is in their conclusions: they resolve in the former to 'me' and in the latter to 'myself'. The 'me' in 'Windlady' is the rain doll. The'Wind / me' conjunction is a natural / magical occurrence that the emblem's drawing illustrates. In 'Windyard' the movement to the final word, 'myself', is of a different order. Reminiscent of the play-box metaphor that we encountered previously, in 'Windyard' the poem's speaker constructs the conditions for the wind, sea, earth and sun to enter his world. We suspect that the 'windyard' was there already in the form of a barnyard or backyard, and that the well, house and stove were also there; and further, that the speaker's imagination transformed them into attractive lodgings for the four elements. Recalling Frye's phrase 'a literalist of the imagination' to describe Blake as believing that the literary artist redeems the fallen world by transforming it into a human shape, we note that the four elements come 'Barking, meowing, talking and carolling'. The poet's characterization of the elements as wind: dog, sea: cat, earth: girl, and fire: bird, now extends to the elements' becoming talkers in their own languages. The universe grows eloquent through the poet's active perception of it and through his art. Not only that, but perceived correctly, the poet's 'myself' is truly the world.

Listen to the Wind is both simple and complex. (Complementary, excellent summaries of the work are provided in J. Stewart Reaney's and Alvin Lee's studies of Reaney, permitting us to focus here only on the most relevant details.) On the simplicity side of *Listen to the Wind,* the play's script calls for sparse staging with only a few props. Jay Macpherson's review of the first production, at London's Althouse College Auditorium in July 1966, describes what the house saw:

> This production can fairly be taken as definitive. More money, more experienced actors, would most likely lessen its peculiar force. It is performed on a stage almost empty except for four chairs, a ladder, and a long table on which props are laid out. (4)

Appropriately for a play built on the foundation of imaginatively listening, sounds of many kinds are featured. Macpherson continues:

> On the stage at the right sit three musicians with piano, percussion and guitar and fourteen chorus members.... The music, composed or put together by the excellent teenage musicians we see on stage, and the sound effects contributed by the chorus, provide half the life of the play. The chorus mime, recite, sing, thump, clap, and play instruments from recorder to pop bottle.... (4)

The chorus, then, is responsible for bringing to life the play's numerous imaginary settings and events. That the chorus is permitted limited resources emphasizes the need for their active involvement, along with the other actors and the audience, in creating *Listen to the Wind.*

Although the multiple stories enacted in *Listen to the Wind* are organized by the Winds that emblematize phases of the mythopoeic cycle, just the way 'Windlady' and 'Windyard' are organized, the renewal that takes place in *Listen to the Wind* is less distinct. Because two opposed endings are enacted in the 'Caresfoot Court' play that Owen and his cousins devise, the revitalization's effect on the play's 'real world' story seems ambiguous. Nevertheless, Reaney's artistic method with the 'Windlady' emblem, the 'Windyard' poem, and *Listen to the Wind* is consistent. In his 'Production Notes' for *Listen to the Wind* he states this system in two different ways, both well worth our attention:

> Art is made by subtracting from reality and letting the viewer imagine or 'dream it out', as Owen is told to in the play.... Words,

> gestures, a few rhythm band instruments create a world that turns Cinerama around and makes you the movie projector[1]....

The illustration and text of 'Windlady' both radically simplify the world and call the reader to imagine the connections between the emblem's visual image and words, resulting in an experience of renewal that is parallel to that of the rain doll and the spiralling wind. The 'Windyard' poem similarly creates an apocalyptic transformation, as we have seen, changing the poems' readers into Blakean projectors, not passive screens comparable to John Locke's blank slates. The play's title, *Listen to the Wind,* is synonymous with Reaney's expression 'dream it out'. In 'Windlady' we hear the rain doll speak to the wind. The play directs its audience to perform, to 'listen to the wind' along with Owen and the other characters who create the plays onstage.

The complexity of *Listen to the Wind* is mostly in the plotting, since two plays take place at once, circling, one inside the other. The outer play tells the story of Owen, a boy who lives in Perth County, Ontario, in the 1930s, and his three cousins, Jenny, Harriet and Ann, who visit him for the summer. Owen is ill, apparently suffering from 'nerves' caused by the separation of his parents. We learn about this nervous malady from Owen when he explains that on his doctor's orders, as a curative he is smoking a pipe — possibly the most surpassingly inept prescription of all time. After the cousins stop gagging and choking on the tobacco smoke, since they all had to have a puff on the pipe, the four children determine to put on plays for some more wholesome summer fun. Owen has a particular motivation regarding this project, namely that his mother loves plays and she might return to see one that her son and nieces put on. Should she do so, this line of thinking might go, her conscience could be caught by guilt-inducing events in the play, the way Hamlet's uncle Claudius's was, and she might reform her ways (unlike Claudius) and return to be a better mother to Owen. After briefly experimenting with dramatizing a version of *Tarzan,* the children proceed, along with several additional characters, to develop and act out a play that they call 'The Saga of Caresfoot Court', adapted from the Victorian novel *Dawn* by Rider Haggard. This melodrama, a typical romance, involves dastardly deeds of murder and betrayal, an angelic heroine, a dashing hero, fateful coincidences, and not just one, but two endings: one tragic, the second comic. All of these events are governed by the North, South, Night, East and West Winds. Each wind contributes emblematically its characteristics to the plays' intertwined events. The four directional winds bring natural attributes, as well as symbolic personifications. From the North, for instance, along with wilderness cold

> come
> The fierce howling mother and the rain, her doll,
> The black huntsman and his men,
> The wind and the wild, wild rain
> To make the branch tap at my windowpane
> To cry and to tap at my windowpane. (17)

Instead of establishing a threatening atmosphere as the North Wind does, another wind, the Night Wind, brings qualitatively different dimensions to *Listen to the Wind.* This difference is suggested by its being named in reference to time, not spatial directions, as the rest of the winds are. 'The Night Wind' is a poem written by Emily Brontë; it is quoted extensively in *Listen to the Wind.* On a structural level, Reaney's use of this poem indicates a parallel between the four children's dreaming out 'The Saga of Caresfoot Court' in 1930s Perth County, and the four Brontë children, Ann, Branwell, Charlotte and Emily, who played together, writing stories and poems such as 'The Night Wind', at Haworth Parsonage in Yorkshire in the early 1800s. This parallel causes a resonance between the earlier and later historical periods, noticed by *Listen to the Wind* audiences as a contrast in poetic styles. The play thus announces that neither the activity of dreaming out nor the action in the 'Caresfoot Court' material is confined to one place and time. Reaney stresses this point when he entitles Scene 33 of *Listen to the Wind* 'Eternity Chorus', and has the onstage Chorus members begin their recital of part of 'The Night Wind' not with the work's original title, but with the word 'Eternity' (88). The stylistically archaic words quoted from the 'Night Wind' poem in the Chorus's arrangement reveal the poet listening to this wind, the wind of inspiration.

Eternity

I sat in silent musing,
The soft wind in my hair,
'O come,' it sighed so sweetly,
'I'll win thee 'gainst thy will.'

'Have we not been from childhood friends?
Have I not loved thee long?
As long as thou hast loved the night
Whose silence wakes my song.'

'And when thy heart is laid at rest
Beneath the churchyard stone
I shall have time enough to mourn
And thou to be alone …'

The Night Wind The Night Wind The Night Wind (89)

These lines present an image of the wind's ravishing the poet, causing her to bring forth the poem out of night and death. The situation is analogous to that in *Listen to the Wind*, where all of the dark machinations in the outer and inner plays move towards Owen's and the audience's imaginative renewal. The final wind to make its presence felt in *Listen to the Wind* is the West Wind, bringing with it the Spring.

In the Chorus's description of the North Wind, did you notice that as a mother the North Wind brings a rain doll? The East Wind, another bitterly cold wind, also brings with her rain and a rain doll (94). Under the influence of the East Wind, Owen's parents together briefly try to relieve his fever by giving him 'something to drink'. When he 'recovers from his fit', Owen says,

> Mother and father. It is time that you two are together again. I felt you both touching me … like rain. (109)

The parents' reconciliation does not last, though, and Owen's nervous condition persists. Perceiving the North and East Wind's rain dolls side by side with the rain doll in 'Windlady' deepens the sense of the spiralling wind's blackness in the emblem, the wildness out of which the land's redemption eventually grows. In *Listen to the Wind,* as mentioned, the recovery is ambiguous.

There is another important doll with similar, though less weather-oriented functions in *Listen to the Wind.* This doll contributes a sinister uncanny element to the 'Caresfoot Court' play. Before the doll appears, the atmosphere is established by Devil Caresfoot, the wealthy owner of the Caresfoot estate, when he exclaims to his son Piers that a table near where they are standing is the very one on which his (Devil's) mother had lain in her coffin, on the first of May fifty years before, and that people had strewn blackthorn branches over the coffin. A southern English belief is that blackthorn branches were used to make Christ's crucifixion crown, and that to bring it indoors is foolhardy because blackthorn in a house augurs that a death there will before long ensue. In this scene, Piers is forced to admit that against his father's explicit directive, he has married Claudia Van Yorick, a servant now pregnant with Piers's child, instead of Maria Lawry, a local landowner whose holdings Devil Caresfoot covets for his family estate. Because of this disobedience, Devil has cut Piers out of his will in favour of Piers's cousin Douglas. Douglas has secretly had a child with Geraldine, another devilish figure who lives at the edge of the forest 'like a gypsy' (29). Because Geraldine had also attracted the amorous attentions of Attorney Eldred, and she wished to accept his marriage proposal, Geraldine killed her baby girl. This baby haunts Geraldine, to the extent that she digs up the body and scatters the bones. The ghost of the baby does not relent, however, instead instructing Geraldine to sew up her wishbone into a doll and give it to Piers and Claudia's baby daughter, Angela. The ghost says to Geraldine,

> Sew up my bone into a doll. Give it to her when she's grown up a bit. And if she loves me and kisses me then I'll have rest for I'll have found my true mother and then I'll not haunt you any more.
>
> GERALDINE: I'll sew your wishbone into a doll, my bonny child, but I cannot find where I threw it.
> GHOST: *laughing* Over here mother. Down the crooked path. Here

> at the weasel's den. Here in your crooked heart. Haste mother for the dawn comes and then I can speak no more.

With a pedigree like that of the doll, it's no wonder that both Angela and Martha, her nursemaid at Caresfoot Court, hate the thing. Nevertheless, Angela does keep it, baby's collarbone and all.

The type of magic at work here is a branch of 'sympathetic magic', called 'contagious magic', which Sir James George Frazer, in *The Golden Bough,* defines as magic based on the principle that 'things which have once been in contact with each other continue to act on each other at a distance after the physical contact has been severed.' In *Listen to the Wind* the doll threatens Angela on behalf of Geraldine, the latter endeavouring to forward Douglas's ambitions against Angela's father, Piers; through its proximity to Angela, the angel of Caresfoot Court, and containing the murdered baby's wishbone, the doll also serves to pacify the ghost. Frazer is quite scathing about this sort of thinking, calling it 'extremely simple and elementary', and familiar 'to the crude intelligence not only of the savage, but of ignorant and dull-witted people everywhere.' Be that as it may, such magic is also deeply entrenched in much of our 'civilized' symbolic thought, for instance when something closely associated with another entity is made to stand for it, such as using the word 'Ottawa' metonymically to designate the entire Canadian government.

The doll reappears near the end of the 'Caresfoot Court' play, as the just deserts are being meted out. The relationship between Angela and her true love Arthur has been treacherously manipulated by Geraldine, again on behalf of Douglas, who is actually blackmailing her to do so, on the threat of exposing her crime of murdering their child. Geraldine's perniciousness seems to be contained in the doll, and, working as a sort of Voodoo doll, in Angela's possession it threatens to destroy Angela. When Arthur learns that his betrothed Angela has married her cousin Douglas the day before his return to Caresfoot Court, he confronts her, and she is holding the doll (124). In Angela's arms, the doll is an emblem of Geraldine's corrupting powers, yet, being the angel she is, Angela insists on interpreting the doll at least partially in a benevolent light. When she realizes how Geraldine and Douglas have tricked her into betraying Arthur, Angela says,

> The doll looks at me! Now I know why she gave it to me. So I would have something when she had stripped away everything and everyone else. (127)

Not great company, perhaps, but better than none, she believes. Angela's good will towards the doll directly leads to the murdered child's redemption in the comic ending of the 'Caresfoot Court' play. Instead of dying, as she does in the tragic ending, Angela wakes from a faint, and feels the influence of the West Wind, asking that it 'help me free the prisoner, the river frozen in the jail of winter' (135). She then asks Martha to bring the doll, indicating that the 'prisoner' is the murdered baby, and more broadly, the play's entirely disordered situation. Angela's love for the doll transcends Geraldine's Voodoo-like evil influence, permitting the comic clarification of relationships that closes the play. Speaking to Geraldine, the ghost of the murdered baby says,

> Evil mother. Cruel murderess. I speak from beneath the snow. Your wish [to die] is granted. You've been a wolf in the forest twice times seven years and now you will be freed....
>
> *Angela kisses the doll.*
>
> For at last someone good enough has been found to kiss the rag doll you made of my bones, loving enough to lick the sores of Lazarus, and gentle enough to weep for the scorpion. Farewell. I have found at last my true mother.
>
> *The West Wind blows and lights the Evening Star.* (136)

Even through all of the melodramatic complexities, we perceive that a renewal is taking shape. Like the rain doll in 'Windlady', the rag doll in *Listen to the Wind* symbolically brings about the recognition of new life at hand. Reaney's 'Production Notes' give us his perspective on Rider Haggard's novel *Dawn,* the main source of 'The Saga of Caresfoot Court':

> It's a melodrama but it still affects me very powerfully because the patterns in it are not only sensational, but deadly accurate. This is a world. Give into its rules a bit, and you'll find that it guides you out of the abyss we live in.... My play is about young people who put on Rider Haggard's *Dawn* because of its strong pattern.

In the 'Windlady' emblem the 'deadly accurate' pattern is more frugally elaborated than it is in *Listen to the Wind.* Still, seeing the emblem and the play arrayed according to the magnetic force they create when brought together serves to intensify the effects of both works of art.

---

1. 'Cinerama' is a wide-screen filming and projection technique developed in the early 1950s. Unfortunately for Reaney's analogy, the showing of Cinerama films involved the use of three projectors.

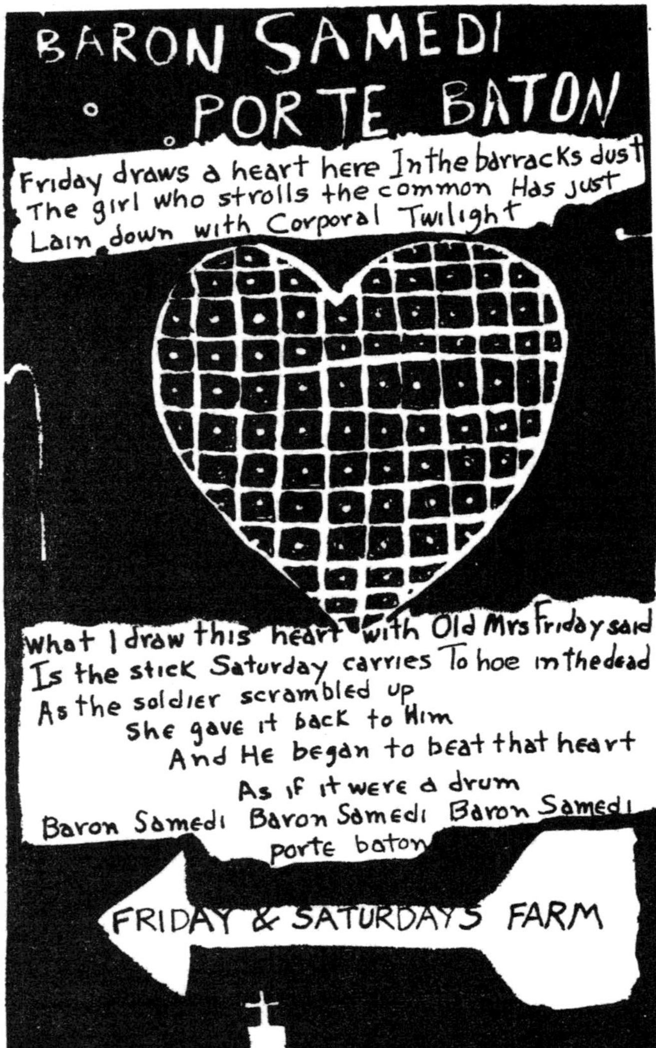
BARON SAMEDI
PORTE BATON
Friday draws a heart here In the barracks dust
The girl who strolls the common Has just
Lain down with Corporal Twilight
What I draw this heart with Old Mrs Friday said
Is the stick Saturday carries To hoe in the dead
As the soldier scrambled up
She gave it back to Him
And He began to beat that heart
As if it were a drum
Baron Samedi Baron Samedi Baron Samedi
porte baton
FRIDAY & SATURDAYS FARM

Baron Samedi Porte Baton

In English this emblem's French title says, 'Baron Samedi Carries a Stick'. The white-on-black illustration features the heart shape we have seen before. As a whole, the emblem represents an excursion on Reaney's part into another galaxy of symbols, Haitian Voodoo. 'Baron Samedi Porte Baton' is not as esoteric as it first might appear. Rather, it seems to be an extension of the rain doll figure, with its sympathetic magic function, into Voodoo as a symbolic system that operates with much the same basic imagery as the mythopoeic tradition. That is, Voodoo's imagery springs from the same sources as those from which are drawn Spenser's and Milton's poetry, Blake's writings, Frye's literary theory, and Jung's alchemically tinged psychology. In a parallel way to that noted with regard to *Twelve Letters to a Small Town,* which uses alchemy as its structural principle, this emblem uses Voodoo imagery and mythology to work out the problems and possibilities created by adapting imported cultures to another place.

In that it was carried from across the ocean and revised to suit local circumstances, Haitian Voodoo is analogous to Canada's immigrant cultures. The anthropologist Alfred Métraux's 1959 book on Haitian Voodoo, which Reaney read,[1] defines Voodoo as 'a conglomeration of beliefs and rites of African origin, which, having been closely mixed with Catholic practice, has come to be the religion of the greater part of the peasants and the urban proletariat of the black republic of Haiti' (15). Voodoo's commingling of symbols, some from 'Catholic practice', the religion of the French colonizers, also takes place linguistically, as Métraux explains:

> The language of Voodoo is Creole, which in Haiti is spoken by everyone except the haute bourgeoisie. It is not a coarse patois, as has often been said, but a comparatively recent language derived

The vèvè of the snake god, Dambellah-wèdo
and his consort Aïda-wèdo. (Métraux 37.)

> from French, just as French is derived from Latin. It has preserved phonetic habits and grammatical structures which, in origin, are clearly African. (22)

The French word *vaudou* means 'an all-powerful and supernatural being', the 'V-God', in Haitian Creole, identified as 'the snake under whose auspices gather all who share the faith' (Métraux 36). This snake is known as Damballah-wèdo. The other snake in the illustration of this *vèvè* is his consort, Aïda-wèdo. The couple also appear as the lower part of the weather vane's shaft in the 'various *loa*' drawing (see page 144). To make its warnings and predictions known, Damballah-wèdo requires a male or female priest, the *hungan* or the *mambo,* to act as an intermediary during ritualistic ceremonies. Participants in the ceremonies are also, however, directly possessed by the various *loa* (spirits), becoming entranced, nearly always dancing, and sometimes trembling and swooning. One method of incarnating particular *loa* — one of whom is Baron Samedi — is for a *hungan* or *mambo* to draw symbols nearby the central post (*poteau-mitan*) on the floor of the sanctuary where a service is being held. Métraux describes this part of the ceremony as follows:

> In Haiti it is the symbolic drawings, called *vèvè,* which fulfil the functions elsewhere devolving upon statues and images. These are traced out, according to the *nanchon* (national or tribal group of the *loa*) of the *loa* whose emblem the officiant wants to represent, in flour made from corn or maize, brick-dust or powdered bark, ashes or even coffee-grounds. (163)

Once the drawing is completed, sacrifices are offered and libations sprinkled to intensify its magic, while prayers are said and rattles are shaken. 'These *vèvè* reveal the presence of the god in tangible form,' Métraux writes. 'These emblematic drawings have a magical nature. Merely by tracing them out the priest puts pressure on the *loa* and compels them to appear. Their function is to summon *loa*' (165). In his book on *Vèvè,* Milo Rigaud relates these ritual diagrams to Hebrew:

> The Hebrew 'vau' or 'vav' — which corresponds to the first syllable of *vau-dou* or *vaudoo* — is therefore the boat in which Legba [messenger of the gods/the Sun] crosses the reservoir. This boat is the voodoo *Azilih* and Hebrew *Aziluth* (Haitian *Erzulie* [Ezili in Métraux]). Consequently, the vèvè or ritual diagrams of voodoo are pronounced and written like *vav* or double v: v-v (vèvè). (74)

Métraux explains that stylistically the *vèvè* themselves share the hybrid nature also characteristic of Voodoo language and rituals:

> Though the *vèvè* are Dahomean in origin their actual style is clearly European, as may be seen from an examination of the accompany-

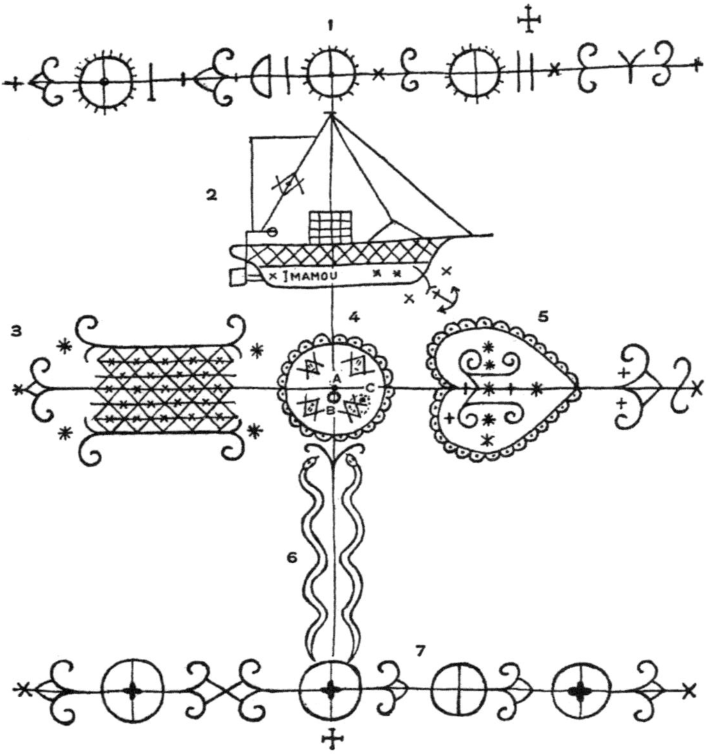

The symbols of various *loa* traced on the ground near a *poteau-mitan*. (Métraux 164.)

ing illustration of 'The symbols of various *loa*'. The scrolls and traceries recall the iron-work and embroidery motifs of the eighteenth century. French inspiration is as evident in them as it is in some of the folklore music and dances. (166)

From the point of view of a Canadian emblematist, several features of Voodoo would be particularly intriguing. In a most pronounced and, according to many, effective way, Voodoo relies on symbolic representations to attract and incarnate its *loa* or spirits. Rigaud compares the *vèvè* to the mandala as 'an astronomical synthesis of the creation' and 'an instrument of psychic magic' (77–78), thus linking Voodoo to Jungian alchemy. Voodoo is a hybrid of European language and Catholicism, along with African, mainly Dahomean, language and religious ideas and practices. Métraux also remarks on a healthy balance in Voodoo which contributes to its 'social utility': 'The faithful find in Voodoo not only a communion with the supernatural, but also an opportunity of amusing themselves. The songs and dances are sacred, but they afford those who indulge in them an altogether profane pleasure' (363–64). Through what Métraux calls its 'intimate union of religion and art' (364), Voodoo is a highly creative force in Haitian society. Métraux writes: 'Not only is it the object of a profound faith but its adepts continually enrich it with fresh contributions both to its mythology and to its liturgy' (365). Perhaps it is particularly in the spirit of this ongoing creativity that Reaney drew on Voodoo as a mythology for this emblem. Certainly the combination of religious and mythological seriousness with pleasurable social interaction is characteristic of Reaney's poetry, fiction and dramatic writing also.

The cultural source of Reaney's 'Baron Samedi Porte Baton' emblem has connotations of mystery, but the emblem's text is based on the by-now familiar mythopoeic cycle, concentrating on fertility that leads to a rebirth from death. The pictures in his emblem are drawn from illustrations in Métraux's *Voodoo in Haiti.* Reaney is using his magnetic method here, bringing into contact symbolic images and text, to see what lines of force are produced.

Baron Samedi is one of the Guédé; the members of this family of *loa* are the spirits who are concerned with the affairs of the dead. The cross (seen at the bottom of Reaney's emblem), Métraux explains, symbolizes Baron Samedi, and partakes of his sacred nature (166). 'The big cemetery crosses or those which crop up around *humfo* [religious centres], consecrated to Guédé, are probably the things which come nearest in Voodoo to tangible representation of a divinity' (166). The cane on the left in Reaney's emblem is Baron Samedi's 'baton', 'the stick Saturday carries to hoe in the dead'. Bringing to mind Reaney's 'Riddle' emblem, as a cane, the stick recalls the third leg of the man about to die in Oedipus's response to the Sphinx's riddle. As a stick, it evokes the lines from the Invocation to the 'Muse of Satire' in *A Suit of Nettles:* 'With Punch's stick (he holds it in his hand) / Beat fertility into a sterile land.'

The left-pointing arrow above the cross in Reaney's emblem might be a simplification of the weather-vane shape that appears in the

The vèvè of the goddess Erzulie Fréda. (Métraux 111.)

'symbols of various *loa*' illustration (page 144); another possibility is that the arrow could be a spade on its side, the spade being a gravedigger's tool and a property of Baron Samedi. As a directional indicator, the arrow points the way to Voodoo's symbolic turning point of the week; when Friday becomes Saturday there is a new beginning.

The heart in Reaney's emblem appears often in Voodoo objects. It can be seen in the 'loa' symbols illustration, and also as the central figure in the *loa* Ezili Fréda's *vèvè* (above). The name Ezili[2] has several related meanings, beginning on a cosmic level with 'the Moon possessed by the Sun'. More concretely, Ezili is the Moon as the Boat which transports the Sun, Damballah-wèdo, across the lake of Night (Rigaud 74). 'Ezili also stands for the planet Venus' (Rigaud 75). In Voodoo she was, then, originally a water spirit, and compared to Aphrodite. She was given the heart as her emblem (Métraux 110). Her day is Friday, the only day that 'the just have sexual relations' (Rigaud 75) — thus, Ezili Fréda.[3] Métraux warns the student of Voodoo not to confuse Ezili Fréda with 'Grande Ezili' (Grandmother Ezili) who is an old woman, reminiscent of Reaney's 'Granny Crack', crippled with rheumatism and only able to walk by dragging herself along on the ground with a stick (112). In Reaney's emblem we find that Friday, Ezili Fréda, who 'draws a heart here in the barracks dust', becomes Old Mrs Friday, who gives the stick to Corporal Twilight. This soldier has just 'lain down' with 'The girl who strolls the common'. This lying down has a double meaning that plays with the Elizabethan metaphor that identifies orgasm and death: 'lain down' in the emblem, then, is sexual and at the same time it is death. From both readings, sex and death, new life emerges. The soldier then begins to 'beat that heart' — the heart that Friday drew 'In the barracks dust' — 'As if it were a drum.'

Reaney's emblem imaginatively identifies Friday's/Ezili Fréda's *vèvè* heart with a drum. From Métraux, we learn that drums are integral parts of Voodoo ceremonies, and in fact, 'The drum is not only a musical instrument, it is also a sacred object and even the tangible form of a divinity.... Like all divinities the drums need men to renew their energy and strength' (182). Reaney's soldier, Corporal Twilight, is resurrected after lying down (in Elizabethan terms, 'dying') with 'The girl who strolls the common'. The soldier then 'began to beat that heart / As if it were a drum,' an imaginative identification of the 'stick Saturday carries' — Baron Samedi's cane / baton — with the drum stick, the ritual tool for renewing the drum as a deity. Reaney's emblem leads us right to the generational core of Voodoo. The baton draws the divine heart *vèvè*, then transforms into a stick to beat the heart, which itself transforms into a sacred drum. The words on the arrow / spade, 'Friday and Saturday's Farm', label all of this magical generating and transforming activity: as occurs on a farm, out of the dead / spirits in the earth arises new life. The parallels with alchemy and biblical mythologies are evident.

If Reaney is drawing on a particular story in his 'Baron Samedi Porte Baton' emblem, it might well be one that Métraux relates concerning Celestina, a *mambo* 'with marvellous "knowledge"', and daughter of Antoine Simon, the Haitian dictator from 1908 to 1910. According to Métraux, 'Celestina, wanting a human heart for a magic rite, caused a soldier of the guard to be disembowelled in front of her. She was seen, dressed in red, walking towards her father's palace carrying the heart on a silver platter.' As at least somewhat of an apologist for Haitian Voodoo, Métraux is outraged by 'this kind of fantasy, which unfortunately Whites are only too ready to believe' (54). Perhaps relishing this gullibility, Reaney did incorporate some of the elements of this gossip in his emblem. In any case, the story is coherent with the theme of sacrificial death leading to new life.

Reaney's libretto for his and John Beckwith's opera *The Shivaree* offers imagery similar to that of 'Baron Samedi Porte Baton': lovers / newlyweds, noise-making and rebirth. Even more strongly attracted by the emblem, though, is another Reaney and Beckwith collaboration, the opera *Taptoo!* This work, like 'Baron Samedi Porte Baton', involves soldiers, drumming, and attempts to 'Beat fertility into a sterile land'. The word 'taptoo' is the root of 'tattoo' in the sense of a drum signal. 'Taptoo' evolved from the Dutch phrase '*doe den tap toe*', meaning 'put the tap to'; in other words, 'shut off' ('Tattoo'). For the British military, Reaney explains in a note to the opera, 'taptoo' names: 'a) the final military signal of the day, announcing the shutting off of taps in the taverns and the return of troops to their quarters and also b) the elaboration of this into a parting song-and-dance entertainment' (*Scripts* 358). Along with 'Baron Samedi Porte Baton', in terms of the mythopoeic cycle of birth, fall, redemption, apocalypse, the purview of *Taptoo!* is struggling to escape the fallen world of death and destruction. Whereas the beating heart / drum in 'Baron Samedi Porte Baton' promises fertility, *Taptoo!* is gloomier than the emblem; it is set in a world of war after war with only a few hints of possible redemption. To obey the taptoo's warning is to shut off the party and go to sleep. In reasoning that awakening follows sleep, perhaps the optimist might find some redeeming quality.

Much as 'Baron Samedi Porte Baton' prompts us to use our wit in order to interpret the emblem's meanings, right in the opening scene *Taptoo!* presents a situation that requires such active emblematic thinking. With variations, this event is re-presented on several occasions later in the opera, a musical and visual motif indicating that it is a key theme of *Taptoo!* The opera opens with two drummers tapping signals; then a mob enters, '*serenading an effigy of King George III they have tarred and feathered*' (304). The setting is during the American revolution, outside a large tent. The rebels show off 'revolutionary symbols' such as a rattlesnake and the Masonic symbol of a triangle containing a large eye, and with mottoes that emphasize violence directed towards the British. Against this frightening backdrop of sight and sound, young Seth is filling a tub with water, quickly intensifying the malevolent curiosity of the mob. Here are the stage directions:

> *In front, Seth plays at a naval battle between a British and Yankee pair of ships, using bellows to propel the toy boats around the tub and a squirt gun to sink them.* (305)

Seth's game functions to elaborate the historical war situation, including introducing contemporary language through the game:

> Lookout reporting
> Privateer to larboard
> Under false colours....
>
> All men on deck!
> Yankee rebel, I suspect!

The mob *does* pick up on the 'false colours' and 'rebels' terminology, and becomes ever more threatening to Seth and his family, who have joined him onstage. Mr Harple asks his son Seth, who is preoccupied with his water pistol and toy boats, to 'desist/From such/A warlike/Game.' Mr and Mrs Harple are Quakers, non-violent to the extent of declining to participate in warfare, and of refusing to pay homage to any earthly authorities represented by such objects as flags, crowns and uniforms. The emblematic meaning of the child's playing at war and the adults' taking his game so seriously is that war is an immature approach to addressing disagreements. Instead of envisioning warfare in its eternal perspective, the adults' war-making turns them into utterly destructive idiots.

On the other hand, *Taptoo!* also reveals the nature of the optimism that attended the establishment of Upper Canada in the early 1790s. Many of the founders of this British colony had remained loyal to Britain and, leaving their first North American homes, moved away from the rebellion of the thirteen colonies against Britain and in the 1770s and 1780s settled in areas of present-day Ontario.[4] *Taptoo!* presents a group of these loyalists as identifying their refuge in biblical terms, sung to the tune of Daniel Read's 'Windham', a religious song with a similar but more generally expressed theme:

> Exiles are we
> Who in 1783
> Walked up from the Mohawk Valley
> To the border river of Niagara.
> Crossing Jordan into promised lands,
> We came in our thousands. (330)

The entry into a promised land is, of course, analogous to a rebirth. The 'Baron Samedi Porte Baton' emblem, with its Voodoo adaptation of Hebrew language and symbolism, is a variety of this analogous thinking. Also, as we noted particularly in connection with the 'Farm' emblem, renewal develops out of conflict; in the *Taptoo!* instance, the conflict is war, a type of death from which a new society, Upper Canada, emerges.

'Baron Samedi Porte Baton' magnetically draws out of *Taptoo!* another key feature of the redemptive journey to the promised land of Upper Canada: sticks. The loyalists' song continues:

> Before we left for these wilderness roads,
> We cut ourselves some ox-goads....
> From the Balm of Gilead tree by the house where I was bred....
>
> Those sticks we drove our oxen with.

The mention of 'wilderness' calls to mind the wandering of the Jews before they reached Israel. Through its name, the Balm of Gilead tree also alludes to several Bible passages, Gilead being one of the regions of the promised land that God showed to Moses (Deuteronomy 34). Since the Balm of Gilead tree itself, *Populus candicans,* is native to North America, and its common name is a transplantation, this mention in *Taptoo!* forms an ingenious parallel to the system of analogies on which the opera is based, namely the enacting of biblical patterns in North American settings, while generating the spiritual biblical meanings, in this case, redemption as an outcome of suffering.

Analogously to beating the heart drawn on the earth, Ezili Fréda's *loa,* as Corporal Twilight in 'Baron Samedi Porte Baton' does in order to stimulate fertility, the loyalists' sticks drive their oxen in order to bring about a transformation from the death of war to the life of creating a human society in Upper Canada. *Taptoo!* makes explicit in words sung by all the identity of these sticks, including Baron Samedi's baton, with the tree of life:

> Those sticks we drove our oxen with:
> We planted them up here in our youth,
> And watered them with our exile's tears.
> Have they withered with the passing years....
>
> No, just as we have, they've taken root,
> Oh so slowly new leaves show,
> And with any luck perhaps we'll grow
> And flourish and bear fruit.

Out of the soil, reaching to the sky, these trees will grow and bear fruit, just as the earthy sexuality and Ezili Fréda's heart that is drawn and drummed in the dust point towards renewed fertility in 'Baron Samedi Porte Baton'.

Related to this role of sticks, marriage is another prominent motif in *Taptoo!* Encompassing several instances of human marriage is the overall situation of the failed marriage of England with its thirteen colonies. Even this large-scale marriage, though, could be interpreted positively, on the basis that the offspring are the United States and Canada.

On the individual human level the first couple introduced are the Quakers, Mr and Mrs Harple. The man's name is Jesse. The Bible's Book of Isaiah articulates a prophecy that is often interpreted as forecasting the coming of Jesus:

> 1.) And there shall come forth a rod out of the stem of Jesse, and a Branch shall grow out of his roots:

> 2.) And the spirit of the LORD shall rest upon him, the spirit of wisdom and understanding, the spirit of counsel and might, the spirit of knowledge and of the fear of the LORD;
> 3.) And shall make him of quick understanding in the fear of the LORD: and he shall not judge after the sight of his eyes, neither reprove after the hearing of his ears:
> 4.) But with righteousness shall he judge the poor, and reprove with equity for the meek of the earth: and he shall smite the earth: with the rod of his mouth, and with the breath of his lips shall he slay the wicked.
> 5.) And righteousness shall be the girdle of his loins, and faithfulness the girdle of his reins. (Isaiah 11:1–5)

The 'rod' that comes forth from the stem of Jesse in *Taptoo!* is Seth, whose name is that of Adam and Eve's third son, a replacement for the sons whom they lost. Seth in *Taptoo!* is the name of the Harples' son and of his son. Both are types of Jesus, the man of God who will execute the last judgment with wisdom and righteousness. About Seth Senior we can learn more from the Isaiah passage. It continues:

> 6.) The wolf also shall dwell with the lamb, and the leopard shall lie down with the kid; and the calf and the young lion and the fatling together; and a little child shall lead them. (Isaiah 11:6)

Seth Senior married Atahentsic, the daughter of the Maumee Chief Turtle. In terms of the Isaiah prophecy, this marriage is a human instance parallel to the unions of wild with domestic animals. In *Taptoo!* General Mad Anthony Wayne does go berserk when he finds out about Seth's marriage to Atahentsic, precipitating their move to Upper Canada, along with their son Seth. Seth Junior, as mentioned, reveals the folly of war by miniaturizing sea battles in a tub, a demonstration of his Christ-like wisdom and righteous judgment.

A third important marriage in *Taptoo!* is that of the English Lieutenant-Colonel John Graves Simcoe (1752–1806) and Elizabeth Posthuma Gwillim (1762–1850). Simcoe was the dynamic commander of the Queen's Rangers during the Revolutionary War, and later on was appointed Upper Canada's first Lieutenant-Governor. In *Taptoo!* Simcoe is portrayed sympathetically, as instrumental in developing life in the colony, as is Elizabeth, his wife. There are overtones in the opera of this couple's corresponding to Adam and Eve as they were both before and after the Fall. In contrast, the opera presents the American rebel General 'Mad Anthony' Wayne as satanic, a racist fool. The Simcoes, far from being eager to slaughter the native peoples, as Wayne is, are officially allied with many of them, and personally involved with individuals. Emblematic of this cooperative relationship, the fourth scene of Act 2, 'Loyal She Began', has Governor Simcoe renaming several features of Upper Canada, with assistance from a First Nations woman, Atahentsic, and her husband Seth's father.

(*On the floor a map of southern Ontario is projected.*)
SIMCOE: And what is this part of the 'bush' called?
ATAHENTSIC: Colonel Simcoe, it is called Wawanosh.
SIMCOE: Let's call it Kent County. And this?
SETH SENIOR: Sir, the Canadians call it Côte de Misère.
SIMCOE: Ah yes, well, we will call it — Essex County. This river?
ATAHENTSIC: Askunessippi.
SETH SENIOR: The French called it La Tranche.
SIMCOE: We shall call it — the Thames. And at the forks here we shall build our new capital New London.

From our perspective now, we could be outraged by Simcoe's insensitive colonialism as demonstrated by his arbitrarily replacing traditional Indian and French (Canadian) names with English names. However, the opera's emphasis is not on this chauvinism, but rather on the renewal process, the Simcoes' attempt to create a peaceable kingdom. As noted, the contrast with Mad Anthony Wayne's racist brutality in *Taptoo!* helps to mitigate our negative judgments about the Simcoes. (One of Governor Simcoe's first legislative acts in Upper Canada was to abolish slavery in the colony.) Also on the affirmative side, after the naming sequence just quoted, Atahentsic and Elizabeth Simcoe interact in a significant way. On the advice of Atahentsic, Elizabeth's mosquito bites are healed by the local plant called 'Touch-me-not'; and she does not try to change the names of places she visits. She learns from the native woman, even though it is difficult for her. The following exchange is typical:

ATAHENTSIC: That is the roaring of Niagara. We are walking by Ontario, the beautiful lake. (*Niagara roar grows fainter.*)
MRS SIMCOE: Ah! Quite like the sea sometimes off Devon in England, only —
ATAHENTSIC: Only what, Mrs Simcoe?
MRS SIMCOE: Only it lacks the marine smell. Atahentsic, will there be rattlesnakes this way?

Mrs Simcoe needs to relate the 'new world' to her English frame of reference, but at the same time she does accept places and things as they are, as they have already been named. An Eve figure, Mrs Simcoe partakes of the fruits of the Edenic world, indicating that the Upper Canada project must go through the mythopoeic cycle beginning with the fall from paradise into our world of time and space, and the search for redemption.

Mrs Simcoe's interest in snakes also echoes Eve's in the Garden of Eden. And with our knowledge of the background to the 'Baron Samedi Porte Baton' emblem, her mention of rattlesnakes becomes especially remarkable. We recall that the 'V-gods' of Voodoo, Damballah-wèdo and his consort Aïda-wèdo, are represented as snakes (see page 142). These are the gods that control fate, and let their intentions be known through their *loa,* such as Baron Samedi. When Atahentsic and Mrs Simcoe do encounter a rattlesnake, on Niagara's Table Rock, their conversation goes this way:

MRS SIMCOE: Ah! Table Rock! The more dangerous a landscape is, the more picturesque! Atahentsic, my dear, do you really think you should pick up that dangerous rattlesnake?
(*Rattling sound as Atahentsic lifts up a rattlesnake above her head.*)
ATAHENTSIC: Yes, Mrs Simcoe, you have never seen a live one before, have you?
MRS SIMCOE: No. (*rapidly taking out sketchbook*)
ATAHENTSIC: Look, Mrs Simcoe, look!
MRS SIMCOE: Now that is the most picturesque thing I've ever seen in British North America!

(*She sketches as she walks backward in front of the majestic advancing Atahentsic and rattling snake.*)

This conclusion to Scene 4, Act 2, gathers into an emblem: a North American woman and animal juxtaposed with a European woman. Mrs Simcoe does not flee in fear from the woman with a snake, as many people might, but instead sketches them. The word 'picturesque' lets us know that Mrs Simcoe is a woman of her time, caught up in the contemporary European aesthetic fashion of the picturesque as distinct from the sublime and the beautiful.[5] The picturesque approach to art was characterized by a preference for painting rough and complex landscapes; its leading English proponent was William Gilpin. In *Taptoo!* it is not so much that Mrs Simcoe finds Table Rock, the native woman, the rattlesnake and the Falls picturesque per se, but that she sketches them — turns the world around her into art. She was also a diarist, verbalizing her surroundings. As we know, like Mrs Simcoe's contemporary, the 'literalist of the imagination' William Blake, Reaney also believes that the way to redeeming the fallen world is to humanize it, actively to imagine it by making verbal and visual art. Governor Simcoe's naming of Upper Canadian places could also be interpreted in light of this transformative process.

Another aspect of the rattlesnake imagery relates to the Finale of *Taptoo!* In the opera's first scene the word 'rattlesnake' is shouted by the

The Gadsden Flag, popular during the American Revolution.

American mob persecuting Jesse and Mrs Harple and their son Seth. The rebels demand that Jesse remove his hat as a sign of respect for 'the emblem of our state', the rattlesnake. As a Quaker, Jesse refuses, and the mob burns down the family's house. When we consider Mrs Simcoe's reaction to the rattlesnake held for her by Atahentsic along with the rebels' symbol of defiance, we can take the scene to mean even more than we have just seen, Mrs Simcoe's imaginatively perceiving and sketching a local reptile. Her sketching the rattlesnake humanizes it, changes its threatening rebelliousness into art. One of the last forts that the British surrendered to the Americans at the end of the rebellion, this one under Lieutenant-Colonel Simcoe, was called 'Fort Defiance'. The British were refusing to give up nine forts on American soil until, as Simcoe puts it in *Taptoo!* the 'Yankees pay our Loyalists for their land' (338), a claim that included the Indian allies of the British. As a theme, then, defiance is turned upside down in *Taptoo!* From the Americans' defying British rule as the backdrop to most of the opera, near the conclusion we have Simcoe's heroic defiance of the Yankees. The final image of the play is a sombre reiteration of this defiance; it emphasizes the Upper Canadians' ongoing struggle for redemption. In a near-repetition of the opera's opening scene, the Finale features Seth, young again, playing with his war toys. This time in the tub British ships are being threatened by American ships, playing out the United States' government's intention of taking over Canada. Here is the last sentence of the opera's concluding stage direction, as the light fades on the younger Seth:

> *Last image is the boy's defiant face, a toy ship in either hand, young scion of an endangered baby colony.* (356)

Within a few years, in 1812, this menace would materialize. To reflect on 'Baron Samedi Porte Baton' is to become aware of an increased urgency for renewal in both the emblem's cosmic movement and the opera's historical circumstances.

---

1. Telephone conversation with Reaney, 26 April 2002.

2. 'Ezili' is the way Métraux spells this name. It can be spelled in several other ways, including, as the *vèvè* shows, 'Erzulie.'

3. I am using the spellings of the various names as reported by Métraux. In other texts, such as Rigaud, the names are spelled differently.

4. Lower Canada, present-day southern Quebec, New Brunswick, Nova Scotia and Prince Edward Island, also received many such settlers who were loyal to Britain. (From 1763, when Britain acquired French territories in North America, until 26 December 1791, the area which would become Upper and Lower Canada was known simply as Québec.)

5. For a fuller understanding, Glickman's analysis of the picturesque and the sublime in Canada is most useful.

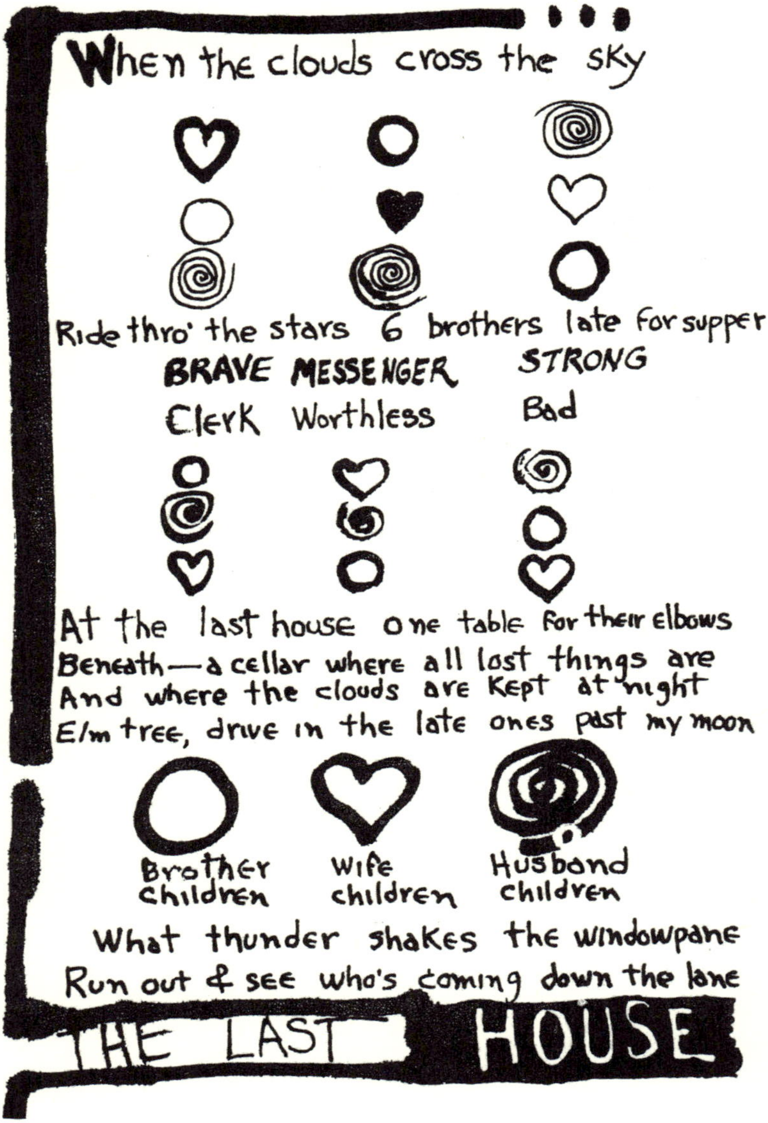
When the clouds cross the sky
Ride thro' the stars 6 brothers late for supper
BRAVE MESSENGER STRONG
Clerk Worthless Bad
At the last house one table for their elbows
Beneath—a cellar where all lost things are
And where the clouds are kept at night
Elm tree, drive in the late ones past my moon
Brother children
Wife children
Husband children
What thunder shakes the windowpane
Run out & see who's coming down the lane
THE LAST HOUSE

The Last House

'The Last House' is Reaney's emblematic announcement of the imminent coming of Apocalypse. The tripartite figure of 'The Riddle' again appears in 'The Last House', middle of the top row, this time along with five variations. The circle, heart and spiral elements which form in 'The Riddle' a symbolic 'Man', are shuffled in 'The Last House', then systematically dealt out in threes, arranged in the emblem like a mystical spread of cards. Rhoda Kellogg would call these variations on basic shapes 'aggregates' (52–63). As we have seen, many of Reaney's emblems are aggregates of the basic heart, circle, spiral and rectangle shapes; 'The Farm': rectangle; 'Baron Samedi Porte Baton': heart; 'Windlady': spiral; and the next emblem we will consider, 'The Hat': circle. The circle also figures in 'Egypt', as does the triangle, which appears as a pyramid; and 'Within Within' combines the triangle with circles and squares. As aggregates, the pictures and the texts take readers/viewers in far-flung directions. Nevertheless, the basic shapes supply the emblems' principle of structural unity. Looking only at the drawings, the visual movement from top to bottom of the emblem is one of complexity resolving into its component circle, heart and spiral.

This winnowing out of the basic shapes is a type of the biblical last judgment as prophesied in the Book of Revelations, when God in the form of Jesus devastates the fallen world in order to bring about the New Jerusalem, the final renewal. Prefiguring this last day, during Jesus's trial one of his judges commanded him to 'tell us whether thou be the Christ, the Son of God.' Jesus responded, 'Hereafter shall ye see the Son of man sitting on the right hand of power, and coming in the clouds of heaven' (Matt. 26: 63–64). These are the clouds 'that cross the sky' over the emblem's last house. Reaney's use of the word 'cross' in this context reveals once again, startlingly but not unexpectedly, his linguistic precision.

Corresponding to the movement of the emblem's illustrations, the eschatological text of 'The Last House' joins sky images — clouds and stars, the moon and thunder — with earth images — a cellar, a house and a lane. The elm tree outside and the table inside the last house are the intermediaries of this sky-earth junction. The six emblematic 'men', composed of vertically arranged hearts, spirals and circles, appear to represent the six brothers. They are named, in Spenserian allegorical fashion, 'BRAVE', 'MESSENGER', 'STRONG', 'Clerk', 'Worthless' and 'Bad'. The symbolic labelled shapes separate horizontally in the third tier of illustrations into a partial schematic family tree. As in 'Within Within', looking at clouds constructs a vision in 'The Last House'. The distinguishing of the six brothers by categories is accompanied by the opposite movement, an infolding of elements: the brothers coming home to 'one table', and the clouds being put to bed in the cellar 'where all lost things are'. The text's closing couplet — located just above the emblem's title — reveals that the clouds, as noted with Jesus's testimony, were messengers proclaiming a mighty storm. The doubt expressed by the words 'What thunder' suggests that there is more to this thunder than a forecast of stormy weather. The biblical book of Revelations abounds with thunder, most often the voice of God. An example is the apocalyptic voice which John testifies to hearing, 'as the voice of mighty thunderings, saying, Alleluia: for the Lord God omnipotent reigneth' (19.2). Following these hints, the emblem's final line is a direct command to the reader, comparable to the biblical admonition 'Prepare to meet thy God!' (Amos 4:12). Less scripturally and evangelically formulated, the text and drawings of 'The Last House' as a whole work can be interpreted as an enactment of the role of imagination in assisting people to be aware of just how they stand in the process of individuation, as described by Jung, the process of bringing together consciousness and the subconscious into a 'Last House' prepared for rebirth.

'The Last House' vividly presents a sense of anticipation, a time and place just before a momentous revelation, when time and space will be collapsed into eternity. The emblem unites a family that is a symbol for all people who await the arrival of the last judgment. With words and phrases such as 'Ride through the stars', 'last', 'supper', 'drive in the late ones' and 'thunder', the emblem's language calls to mind some of the Bible's major books of prophecy, such as Amos, Ezekiel and Revelations, as well as the Gospel stories of Jesus's last supper, another immediately pre-apocalyptic moment. When we consider these echoes alongside the visual quotations and variations on the illustration of the 'Riddle' emblem in particular, it is evident that quotation is a crucial compositional as well as thematic feature of 'The Last House'.

Which of Reaney's other works are magnetically drawn to 'The Last House' on the basis of their inclusion of quotations? The answer is, a lot of them. Since we have just been discussing *Taptoo!* in the previous chapter, a way to start exploring the topic of quotation is with John Beckwith's article on 'Musical Quotations in *Taptoo!*' in which he also offers insight into Reaney's use of historical quotations in the opera's lyrics. '*Taptoo!* is best described as a documentary ballad opera,' Beckwith writes. He goes on:

> Why 'documentary'? Reaney's libretto mixes imagined characters and characters who actually lived, and it quotes realistically from historical research materials.... In parallel fashion, the musical score refers to eighteenth- and early nineteenth-century American and British military and patriotic music, songs, dances, marches, and hymn-tunes in almost every scene....
>
> It seemed Reaney and I were working towards a continuity where period quotations, both literary and musical, would emerge from the sung story every so often. (6)

Beckwith is delineating a complex magnetizing process here, one that operates between fictional and historical elements of the opera and creates a 'continuity'. The interaction reverses expectations, perhaps, in that rather than the fictional material, the 'sung story', emerging from historical material, according to Beckwith, the opposite seems to occur. Reaney's own musical training, as well as his collaboration with Beckwith, would have made him aware of the potential of quotation to supply meaningful connections at a profound level, not simply as conveyors of a retro atmosphere. In Beckwith's account of how in *Taptoo!* 'period quotations, both literary and musical, would emerge from the sung story', we can see the Blakean principle of the creative power of imagination. Documentary elements are transformed by Reaney and Beckwith's opera, brought back to life by the dramatist and composer's co-operative art.

To focus especially on Reaney's self-quotation, of the kind visually present in 'The Last House', a place to start could be Louis Dudek's haughtily worded essay on Reaney, 'A Problem of Meaning'. Dudek characterizes *One-man Masque* and *Colours in the Dark* as 'little more than ... stage setting[s] for a reading of Reaney's poems' (25). Shortly after the first performance of *One-man Masque*, Reaney recounts the masque's genesis in 'An Evening with Babble and Doodle: Presentations of Poetry'. The essay's subtitle confirms Dudek's comment, obviously without the attempted belittling. Reaney writes that Beckwith had asked him to deliver a poetry reading before the première performance of *Night-Blooming Cereus,* the hour-long opera for which Beckwith wrote and directed the music, and Reaney wrote the libretto. In his 'Babble and Doodle' essay Reaney says,

> I decided that something more than just a reading was called for, and now we come to the doodle part of this story, since I ended up writing another libretto for a masque — masque in the sense of a series of tableaux and spectacles, or stage images. I had been working on a series of poems that presented a subject in various keys: you start out with Dwarf, modulate to a poem about a Baby, proceed to one about a Dauphin (baby Prince) and eventually fly from it all with that baby among the birds — the hummingbird. This suggested a stage picture that started out with a cradle, proceeded through chair, table, bed, rocking-chair to coffin, turned back again through the purgatorial world with rain barrel, hall tree, dresser and mirror, tree branch, ladder and cardboard box. At the beginning of the recital you could put the cradle beside the coffin and at the end of it you could, as the dead child was reborn, take the cradle back again. The poems could be read at different points of this big circle since they too moved in a circle through Life, into the world of Death, coasting perilously near Eternity, then back into the world of Death and so into Life again. I had always observed in poetry readings that the great difficulty was the spaces between poems. If there were no spaces at all the listeners tended to suffer from over intake of image. Moving about from prop to prop would help here but I decided also to write a series of comic and macabre monologues to be performed in between the poems. (42–43)

In connection with the 'Castle' emblem, we have explored the circle inscribed by *One-man Masque.* On the basis of the masque, Reaney would go on to develop *Colours in the Dark* (1969), a play that, as Dudek points out, also includes many quotations from Reaney's own works.

Craig Stewart Walker's study of six outstanding Canadian dramatists suggests that Reaney's recycling of poems in new artistic contexts is motivated by his intending to construct 'a collective memory for the audience'. With this observation, Walker is specifically addressing an occurrence at the November 24, 1973, Toronto première of *Sticks and Stones,* the first play in Reaney's *Donnellys* trilogy. Audiences arriving at the Tarragon Theatre event, Walker writes,

> found the dark walls surrounding them covered with chalk inscriptions in Reaney's own handwriting — phrases and key words from the script, it gradually emerged. These effectively created a collective memory for the audience, substituting theatrical environment for cultural tradition, so that as the play unfolded there was experienced a kind of *déjà vu* (or perhaps *déjà entendu*). (53)

This explanation is plausible, particularly allowing for the time frame involved: arriving at the theatre for a play, reading the material on the walls, then experiencing a performance of *Sticks and Stones.* In the larger context of Reaney's opus it is also possible that readers would have in mind other works by Reaney and recognize as quotations the words in the text before them, thus coming into contact with the text's memory layer. The same could be said about encountering the visual images in 'Two Chapters from an Emblem Book: 1969–70'; the illustration in 'The Last House' strongly reminds us of 'The Riddle'. We are then able to use our understanding of the circle, heart and spiral shapes in 'The Riddle' to help interpret 'The Last House'.

Walker points out that this 'technique was further amplified over the next three years during which the trilogy was premièred, for in the second and third plays, key events, gestures, and words were repeated from the preceding instalments' (53). He comments that the procedure was highly appropriate for the *Donnellys* trilogy 'because of the recurring pattern of moral struggle inherent in their history' (54). Walker's relating of Reaney's 'collective memory' technique to the plot of *The Donnellys,* which involves repetition, is based on the insight that the plays' quoted language corresponds to the repeated events in the onstage action. Considering Reaney's work as a whole, though, there is more to his frequent quoting of his own works than language and plot parallels. To explain the wider significance of these self-quotations, a good entry point is the quoting that we have observed in the emblems, particularly in 'The Last House'. Near the beginning of *Fearful Symmetry*, Northrop Frye reflects on William Blake's work as a whole; he makes some observations that are equally relevant to Reaney's oeuvre, observations that aid in positioning us to understand Reaney's use of self-quotation.

In the first place, what lies behind Frye's effort to consider Blake's work as a whole? Certainly it is not just a matter of the due diligence expected of a doctoral thesis writer. And it is more than a response to Blake's plea that before condemning his works as 'a Madman's Scrawls', people 'do [him] the justice to examine before they decide' (qtd. in *Fearful Symmetry* 4). Having done Blake's poetry this justice, Frye, unlike many Blake critics, realized that spelling out the numerous biblical and other allusions in his work and studying the impacts on Blake of his reading and personal acquaintances were futile as ways to explain his work accurately. Frye writes, 'In the study of Blake it is the analogue that is important, not the source; and even essential sources such as the Bible and Milton are of value only as sources of analogues' (*Fearful Symmetry* 12). An 'analogue' is something that is parallel, similar or equivalent to another thing. For instance, in the Bible, the Israelites' release from captivity in Egypt and reaching the promised land are analogous to spiritual salvation or awakening. Analogical thinking and writing connect objects, people and events along a vertical axis of recurrence or similarity, as distinct from the horizontal axis of narrative, where difference is emphasized. In 'The Last House' the six circle / heart / spiral variations are related analogously to each other, as they are also to the circle / heart / spiral 'Man' in 'The Riddle'. The 'MESSENGER' figure is identical to this 'Man', while the other brothers are variations on the theme, but not progressions, as a new set of shapes could be. This language from the analysis of music is apt, of course, since the same structural dynamics are often at play in musical compositions. We recognize the original theme 'in' variations on it. The 'in' here signifies the paradigmatic relationship that analogy involves.

Adding another dimension to the analogue feature of Blake's writing, Frye comments on Blake's thoroughgoing consistency:

> His principles he held with bulldog tenacity all his life. The lyrics of his adolescence, the prophecies of his middle period, the comments which blister the margins of books he read on a sickbed at seventy, are almost identical in outlook.... Even phrases and lines of verse will reappear as much as forty years later. (*Fearful Symmetry* 13)

We have already remarked Reaney's comparable consistency in his creations over his lifetime. With Blake, as a consequence of such consistency, Frye treats the finished works, those he engraved, as a coherent whole, as did Blake.

> Consistency, then, foolish or otherwise, is one of Blake's chief preoccupations, just as 'self-contradiction' is always one of his most contemptuous comments.
>
> Therefore, if the engraved poems of Blake form a canon, as we have suggested, anything admitted to that canon, whatever its date, not only belongs in a unified scheme but is in accord with a permanent structure of ideas. (*Fearful Symmetry* 14)

Frye's phrase, 'a permanent structure of ideas', can denote also the foundation of Reaney's artistic method, as our study of his emblems and the works magnetically drawn to them has demonstrated. The analogues presented in 'The Last House' serve as a clear instance of Reaney's visual affirmation that although we might be seeing a new or different work, there is a structure of ideas that informs both, a structure that transcends time and space by its presence.

THE HAT

Against me wears the wind a coat
And to protect her from your feet
Ma Earth puts on a dusty shoe
Rain against him taps a roof
Against me puts the Sun a hat

Hey you! Tramp! When is it that
You'll take off your dusty shoes
& hang up your coat & hat

Child, listen: that will be
When in my tramping, weeping, searching

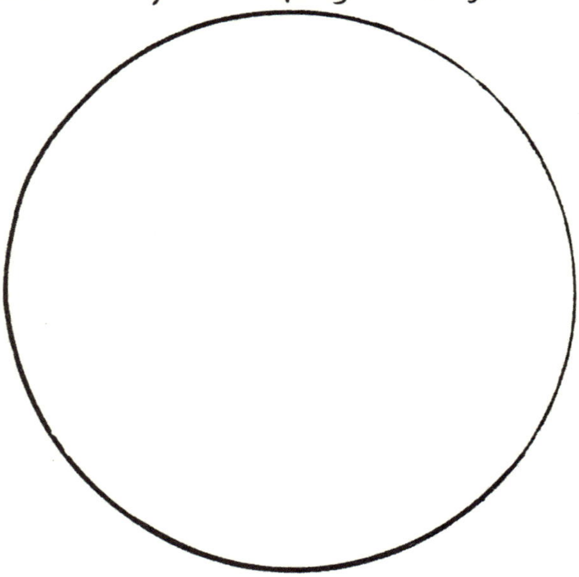

I have found A river to the sea.

The Hat

'The Hat' is the tenth and final emblem of Reaney's 'Two Chapters from an Emblem Book, 1969–70'. Like many of the previously discussed emblems, 'The Hat', and thus the unfinished emblem book itself, brings us around to the threshold of apocalyptic change. Our awareness of this possibility in our individual lives is this emblem's, really the entire series', theme.

The illustration part of 'The Hat' is strikingly plain: a circle, symbol of unity. This visual image carries on with the winnowing process that we noted in 'The Last House', in which the visual movement from top to bottom, from complex to simple, shows the six combinations of shapes resolving into their components, the circle, heart and spiral. In 'The Hat' only the circle remains.

The text of 'The Hat' resumes Reaney's allusive 'quotation and variations' technique that is so vigorously active in 'The Last House'. At the same time, 'The Hat' invites exploration in light of the Jungian model of human development that also, as we have seen, illuminates 'The Castle' and 'The Riddle' particularly.

The emblem's title suggests that we are viewing a stylized hat from above. Jung's analysis in *Psychology and Alchemy* is that the hat, as a covering for the head, has the general sense of something that epitomizes the head. Just as in summing up we bring ideas 'under one head' (*unter einen Hut*, 'hat', in German), so the hat, as a sort of leading idea, covers the whole personality and imparts its own significance to it. Coronation endows the ruler with the divine nature of the sun, the doctor's hood bestows the dignity of a scholar, and a stranger's hat imparts a strange nature (47). The person wearing the hat in Reaney's emblem, then, in accordance with the symbolism of the circle, could be considered to have achieved a state of unity, with what or whom, the emblem's text could make clear.

What role does the person who wears the circular hat in Reaney's emblem play? For a start, the Tramp seems to experience things from an unusual perspective. It is suggested that the person wearing the hat is not the agent; instead, Nature acts, as we learn from the line 'Against me puts the Sun a hat'. This unusually ordered sentence also clearly associates the hat/circle with the sun, as Jung's note about the crown does. In turn, the sun is associated by Jung with the mandala: 'Circumscribing the head, the hat is round like the sun-disc of a crown and therefore contains the first allusion to the mandala' (48). Cirlot's article on mandalas succinctly pinpoints their significance. The mandala is 'an aid in inducing certain mental states and in encouraging the spirit to move forward along its path of evolution from the biological to the geometric, from the realm of corporeal forms to the spiritual' (190). Jung sees this spiritual movement as a stage in the individuation process when archetypal images of unity emerge from the collective unconscious into the chaos of consciousness (27). In this reading, the 'me' who is the Tramp in 'The Hat' is by extension everyone who is at the stage of coming to terms with the contradictions and conflicts in situations that have risen to consciousness. We might recall a similar pattern at work in *One-man Masque,* emblematized in the masque's final display of the man wearing a mandala tray of candles for a hat.

Reinforcing this interpretation of 'The Hat,' the syntax of the emblem's text inverts so-called normal, scientific rationality, which George Grant aptly defines as 'the summoning of anything before a subject and putting it to the question, so that it gives us its reasons for being the way it is as an object' (21). The emblem's syntax effectively upsets the usual subject-as-questioner/object-as-respondent paradigm. For example, a line such as 'Against me wears the wind a coat' displaces conscious time- and space-bound perception, and lets us know that the subject position expressed by the emblem is that from the perimeter, rather than from what we normally conceive to be our position, the point of view at the centre. The Tramp's response to the child's question about 'When' the Tramp's journey will be finished, is phrased, reflexively, in a renewed normal word order. The suggestion is that the Tramp has envisioned the infinite — the view from the circle's perimeter — and is still awaiting a final revelation. The sentence changes an earthly traveller's metaphors to water metaphors, which in turn metamorphose from 'A river to the sea'. This sense of a transformative individuating process is underscored by the sea's symbolic meanings as both the source of life and its goal, birth and death — transitional states of the spirit.

Again it is pertinent to bring into this discussion Northrop Frye's insights. In his 1961 article 'The Archetypes of Literature' he argues that the 'central myth of literature, in its narrative aspect', is the 'quest-myth', of the sort emblematically presented by 'The Hat'. Frye continues, invoking some Jungian imagery as well as sun/hero imagery that is familiar by now:

> Now if we wish to see this central myth as a pattern of meaning also, we have to start with the working of the subconscious where the epiphany originates, in other words in the dream. The human cycle of waking and dreaming corresponds closely to the natural cycle of light and darkness, and it is perhaps in this correspondence that all imaginative life begins. The correspondence is largely an antithesis: it is in daylight that man is really in the power of darkness, a prey to frustration and weakness; it is in the darkness of nature that the 'libido' or conquering heroic self awakes. Hence art, which Plato called a dream for awakened minds, seems to have as its final cause the resolution of the antithesis, the mingling of the sun and the hero, the realizing of a world in which the inner desire and the outward circumstance coincide.... So in terms of significance, the central myth of art must be the vision of the end of social effort, the innocent world of fulfilled desires, the free human society. (18)

Frye's characterizing of day and night, in human experience the states of being awake and dreaming, as 'largely an antithesis', suggests a dialectic process whereby these opposites clash, and by their clashing form a synthesis. In the case of art, the opposition results in 'the realizing of a world in which the inner desire and the outward circumstance coincide'. Reaney's emblem expresses awareness of this process by including both the difficulties of everyday life, represented by the weather, and the possibility for finding the sea of the collective unconscious out of which rises the sun of consciousness. The circle illustration in 'The Hat' is evidently a representation of before and after the individuation process: the circle is a hat, looked at both from above/outside and from inside; it is the familiar sun of daytime weather; and it is the sun of the heroic dreamer awakened.

Along with Jung's concepts, William Blake's thinking about analogies probably influenced Frye's account of what he calls in the passage just quoted 'correspondences' between the subconscious/conscious and night/day. In *Fearful Symmetry* Frye points out that Blake's understanding of analogy critically extends the word's usual sense of indicating 'something that is parallel, similar or equivalent to another thing'. For Blake, Frye writes,

> all images whatever may be symbols of the world of innocence when thought of in terms of eternal existence, and symbols of the world of experience when thought of in terms of death and annihilation. No class of natural images, then, can be identified with either world: prisons belong solely to experience, but a prison is a building, and so is Golgonooza. (382)

(Golgonooza is Blake's imagined 'City of Art' [Bloom 847], a mandala-shaped structure that is described in his most important poem, *Jerusalem.*) For Blake, a prison, a place of vengeance, and Golgonooza, a state of healing and forgiveness, are analogues. They are parallels, but radically opposed, the prison being an inversion of the eternal state. Properly understood, the circle in Reaney's emblem 'The Hat' empowers its wearer with such a two-fold mindfulness, as noted in the discussion of central and peripheral perspectives. Thereby the circular hat also confers on its wearer the possibility to continue the heroic search for 'A river to the sea', in Jungian terms, the quest for imaginative integration and transformation.

Through its use of verbal quotations from Reaney's earlier work, 'The Hat' emblem reveals the figure of analogy both in its more usual form, where the parallel is not an opposition, but is closer to an identification; and in the Blakean form of a radical contrary. As identifications, these quotations of words and word patterns function as allusions in that they recall other contexts, such as the whole poem and the whole plays where the poem's words occur. As oppositions, these quotation analogies express the fallen and the unfallen worlds, Reaney's Age of Dread and Peaceable Kingdom (*Colours in the Dark* 8–9).

Reaney's 1952 poem 'The Tall Black Hat' presents an emblematic figure:

As a child, I dreamt of tomorrow
Of the word 'tomorrow' itself.
The word was a man in a tall black hat.... (*Poems* 101)

The poem goes on to develop this character 'named Sir Thomas Tomorrow', and his brothers, the days that are to come. One brother, the poet dreams, walks towards him 'with his speck of Future / And a tall black hatful of Fate' (*Poems* 102). In linking the future and fate with a person wearing a tall black hat, this early poem provides a partial sense of the theme of the emblem 'The Hat'.

However, the constellation of words that explicitly appears in the emblem 'The Hat' first takes shape in 1959 in the poem 'Granny Crack'.

I was a leather skinned harridan
I wandered the county's roads
Trading and begging and fighting
With the sun for hat and the road for shoes.

You played a pigsty Venus
When you were young, old dame,
In the graveyard or behind the tavern.
The burdock girl was your name.

She talked vilely it is remembered,
Was a moving and walking dictionary
Of slang and unconventional language
The detail of her insults was extraordinary.

We dozen scoundrels laid you
For a quarter each in the ditch
To each you gave the sensation
That we were the exploited bitch.

You saw me freckled and spotted
My face like a killdeer's egg
When, berry-picking kids, you ran from me
Frightened down the lane by the wood.

They saw her as an incredible crone
The spirit of neglected fence corners,
Of the curious wisdom of brambles
And weeds, of ruts, of stumps and of things despised.

I was the mother of your sun
I was the sister of your moon
My veins are your paths and roads
On my head I bear steeples and turrets
I am the darling of your god. (*Poems* 121)

Most readily discernible as verbally analogous, perhaps, are the poem's 'sun for hat and the road for shoes', alongside the emblem's 'Ma Earth puts on a dusty shoe' and 'Against me puts the sun a hat'. Being both an earthy tramp and an earth spirit, the character Granny Crack confers on the poet his power to see doubly. He gains this vision through his perception of Granny Crack herself, for instance in her role as 'a pigsty Venus', an epithet that concisely expresses her double nature, the pigsty and the Venus characteristics being analogous in the Blakean sense of forming contraries. The epithet is itself an analogue, recalling the line from the 'John Dong' song in *A Suit of Nettles,* 'Pigs in the sties of Venus' (49).

'Granny Crack' reveals how the development of the youthful poet's vision is shamefully accelerated by his and his fellow scoundrels' paying 'the burdock girl' for sex. This escapade resulted in the boys' feeling that they were the ones who had been trashed, not the young Ms Crack. ('Crack', by the way, is explained in Reaney's story 'The Ditch' as 'the vulgar farmer way of talking about the difference between man and woman', the former being known as 'pricks' [*Box Social* 23]. The name also recalls the children's chant: 'Step on a crack, break your granny's back.') This seeing doubly constitutes the theme of 'The Hat', where the hat is seen from within and without.

A fourth instance of the Granny Crack material, a scene (Act I, scene 6) in Reaney's 1969 play *Colours in the Dark,* is analogous in another important way to the 'Granny Crack' poem on its own and in *One-man Masque,* and as it figures in 'The Hat'. On a structural level the *Colours in the Dark* scene is an analogue of both the poem and the emblem: all are in the form of dialogues. In *Colours in the Dark* several children ask Granny Crack questions, and she reveals herself to be older than the ice age, and a witness to the ensuing battles of the conifers with the deciduous trees. This 'revealing' takes place verbally, in responses to the children, and also physically, as Granny Crack removes her manifold layers of clothing to hang them on a line, only leaving on her 'seven shrouds', as she says, 'to keep me warm while I tramp the road to heaven' (29).

The first of the seven stanzas of the poem 'Granny Crack' is spoken in Granny Crack's voice. The voice then shifts to the scoundrel boys, who address her for a stanza. The third stanza speaks to the reader in an unspecified voice; then the fourth returns to the boys' addressing Granny Crack. She intervenes in the fifth, telling them that she knew they were afraid of her. The sixth stanza, like the third, is an unidentified voice, the poet's it seems, describing the boys' perspective in the way an impersonal, omniscient narrator might. The seventh, final, stanza is Granny Crack's revelation of her identity as an analogue of the Biblical Whore of the Apocalypse (Revelations 17–18), who, being forgiven, becomes New Jerusalem — 'the darling of your god'.

'The Hat', like 'Granny Crack' is in dialogue form, an exchange between a child and the Tramp. The latter character is an analogue of Granny Crack, who, if she is not the identical figure, is a parallel case, as signalled by the words and theme that the explicitly 'Granny Crack' works share with 'The Hat'. Also analogous, in the term's sense of parallel, is the dialogue form of the works. The dialogues indicate shifts in perspective, and are in turn analogous with all of the works' theme of double mindfulness, the awareness of the Age of Dread as it is on the verge of being swept away apocalyptically, and replaced with the already imagined Peaceable Kingdom.

Reaney's work is replete with instances of analogues. Although most are not Reaney's inventions, his use of them, then his re-use of them as analogues, makes them his own. When we re-encounter a character, an animal, a setting, we perceive the analogical relationship that links the two or more occurrences. We have explored the Granny Crack character; other characters include drummers such as we have found in the muse of satire in *A Suit of Nettles,* in 'Baron Samedi Porte Baton' and *Taptoo!;* the Family Compact who appear in *A Suit of Nettles, Serinette* and *The Boy with an R in His Hand,* for instance; the Brontë children, who on account of their imaginative powers inspired the characters of *Listen to the Wind* and *Zamorna;* father figures, mothers, sons and the list goes on. Particular animals figure in Reaney's work analogously: geese, as in *A Suit of Nettles;* the killdeer, the bird after which one of Reaney's plays is named, and whose eggs turn up often, even, as we've seen, in 'Granny Crack', the vehicle of a simile that constitutes a detail of a self-portrait of James Reaney. Analogues in settings also occur frequently. Southwestern Ontario is the overarching setting, and includes farms, roads, fields, rivers, towns. From one of Reaney's plays to others various simple props reappear: bicycles, stepladders, tables, branches, sawhorses. Finally, to be perceived throughout Reaney's works as analogues are organizational schemes such as the alphabet, numbers, the calendar, lists, plots from fairy stories, and musical keys. All of these formal and thematic analogues weave together to make of Reaney's oeuvre a complex unity, in Frye's phrase, 'a permanent structure of ideas' (*Fearful Symmetry* 14). The visual image and the text of 'The Hat' reveal this unity and permanence emblematically.

An Emblematic Photograph of James Reaney

At this point, we have cycled through all ten emblems in 'Two Chapters from an Emblem Book', and discovered ways in which Reaney's reading and writings are magnetically drawn into the force fields generated by the emblems. We have seen from these emblems and from many of his other works, that endings for Reaney are also beginnings, doors from the past into the future.

With its title, *Windsor Review: A Journal of the Arts;* its illustration, a photograph of James Reaney; and its text imprinted on the photographed book that he is holding, the Spring 1996 *Windsor Review* cover invites being read as an emblem. The torn spine of the book in the photograph has on it the word 'ART'. On the front are the words 'Ontario Teachers' Manuals: ART'; and lower on the cover it says, 'Authorized by the Minister of Education'.[1] (Robert Allan Pyne, a Conservative from Newmarket, was the Minister.) Centred between the lines of text is Ontario's coat of arms. This manual was first published in 1916, reprinted numerous times, and would have been the guide for Ontario's Art teachers when Reaney was attending school in Stratford.

In itself, the manual is emblematic. It is a guide to teaching Ontario's elementary school children, the citizens, including artists, of the future. The manual also points to the past; it claims its authority from being founded on principles developed over centuries. While the manual presents comprehensive lesson plans for use month by month for eight years, nevertheless, the anonymous author says in a General Introduction,

> It is not intended that the Manual should put the words in the teacher's mouth; rather it is intended that these lessons should offer one way of inculcating certain principles that must be taught, in order that each teacher may, after a similar manner, develop an

Front cover of *The Windsor Review*, Spring 1996.

> individual style of teaching. It is just as desirable that the instructor's individuality in teaching should be cultivated as it is that the pupil's individuality of expression in the different mediums should be developed. (19)

These overriding principles range among ethical, cultural and industrial qualities. The students (and their teachers) are permitted individuality in style only. One general principle is described as follows:

> The Course in Colour has been prepared in accordance with the principle that education along any line should proceed as far as possible from the known to the unknown. Throughout the Manual the pupil's mental development has been kept in view as of first importance. (35)

Recalling William Blake's view of 'mystery', as the contrary of revelation, and Reaney's constant drive to 'imagine things out' in words and in art, we can appreciate how repugnant such a principle would be to both of these poet/artists. That children's 'mental development' should proceed towards the 'unknown' is simply bizarre.

To indicate the method of enforcing the children's freedom to have their own styles, the manual supplies a 'Representation' lesson plan that is intended to be a model for all art lessons. After 1) a two- to five-minute demonstration by the teacher of how to do the project, 2) the distribution of materials for one to five minutes, 3) a two-minute individual study of the object to be represented, and oral question-and-answer determination by the whole class of the order in which to proceed with the representation, the students are set to work for five to ten minutes, while 'the teacher passes quietly around noting every important mistake that is being made'. For the next two to five minutes,

> The class stops work, and each drawing is held off and compared with the model, while the teacher mentions the mistakes he has observed and asks those who have made these errors to raise their hands. The drawing of any pupil who does not recognize his mistake should be brought forward so that he may see it beside the model, with which he may then compare it at a better distance.

Even more distressing, perhaps, than the devastating focus on the children's mistakes is the standardization demanded by the teacher. No wonder that the institution where teachers were trained was called the 'normal school'. The lesson proceeds, permitting the children another chance.

> • 5 to 10 min. The pupils correct the drawings where it is possible or begin a fresh drawing on the other side of the paper.
> • 2 min. The drawings approved of for effort or degree of progress.
> • 2 min. The best drawings brought forward to show the class. Attention called to merits, such as good placing, truth of shape, colour, growth, etc., as the case may be.
> • When time permits and interest is still fresh, another sketch may be made. (44)

Not surprisingly, the teacher decrees whose drawings are salvageable, approves the children's amount of 'effort or degree of progress', chooses the 'best drawings', determines the drawings' 'merits', and calculates whether there is time for another round. The implication of such lessons is the teacher's overwhelming authority.

The manual specifies various 'picture studies' in order to develop the children's art appreciation skills. In one of the units on 'Perspective' the picture to be studied is Hobbema's *The Avenue at Middelharnis,* the painting that Reaney's 'Egypt' emblem parodies. (See page 73.) This lesson on perspective was probably the occasion when the 'percheron harness' was fastened on the emblem-maker's eyes, 'Egypt' being his announcement that he could see beyond it.

As well as emblematizing, Janus-like, a doorway between past and future, predominantly signified by the art manual, the cover of the *Windsor Review* presents a portrait of James Reaney. Much of the inside of this issue focuses on Reaney too; it contains an essay about his 'faith in stories', by the *Windsor Review* editor and cover photographer, Marty Gervais; Reaney's poems 'Brush Strokes in Decorating a Fan' and 'To Flow Like You'; an interview with Reaney; a short story of his, entitled 'Memento Mori'; and several of his drawings and sketches. Rather than being biographical in a personal sense, for the most part the *Windsor Review* issue presents Reaney as not only a multi-faceted artist, but also as a teacher, beginning with the emblematic cover photo of him holding the teachers' manual for art.

Germaine Warkentin emphasizes Reaney's role as an educator in her 1972 introduction to his poems, saying that he is 'before all else, a committed teacher' (vii). In her recent essay on *A Suit of Nettles,* she characterizes him as having been, among other things, 'a deeply responsible member of the professoriate at the University of Western Ontario'. I learned that when I was one of his 'Ontario Literature and Culture' students in 1979–80. Marty Gervais's introductory essay in the *Windsor Review's* special Reaney issue also stresses his activities as an effective teacher.

Reaney's response to the 'perspective in art' lesson was to take it as a Blakean contrary: a stage in the process of realizing vision without the harness of traditional perspective's laws. Similarly, he turned upside down the normal-school notion of a teacher as a judgmental authority figure. As we might expect after exploring Reaney's emblems, this process is not simply to reject a contrary in favour of its opposite, but rather, as with 'Egypt', to incorporate the contraries as a whole.

Over the years, numerous people have commented on Reaney's teaching, often focusing on his erudition. Marty Gervais's account of Reaney's 'faith in the "story"' brings out another aspect of Reaney's sharing through his teaching. Gervais comments on Reaney's method of magnetizing ordinary people's knowledge of their own lives, that is, documentary, and imaginative myth:

> Reaney's idea — this approach at asking questions, and researching the material — on the surface may be the stuff of journalism, all this tapping into secrets. But he much preferred the leap into something more visionary, artful, inventive. His decision was to shape these tales, transform them into metaphors, whole plays, poems, pictures, music, anything to illuminate the experience for us all. But not didacticism in a pedestrian way. (1–2)

Nevertheless, didacticism. Through his multiple arts, Reaney teaches. We have experienced this combination of art and teaching in considering his emblems. After all, emblems originated as teaching tools. Gervais goes on,

> When I speak of Reaney's faith, it's in recognizing that each and

> every one of us has a story, something to contribute. Nothing intellectual. Rather, an acknowledgement that at the grassroots, there's an experience that touches everyone. It tells us something about the way we live, think, feel and behave. (2)

Actually, with Reaney there is 'plenty intellectual'. Gervais's point, though, is that his pedagogical approach is not the 'sage on the stage' type, one who drops crumbs from his vast store of knowledge to the ignorant students at his feet, hungry for enlightenment. Reaney's deep knowledge of the classical Greek and Roman periods, the Renaissance, the Romantic and the Modern, in terms of these eras' philosophies, art, theatre, music and poetry appears in his own work, transformed. Reaney's lesson is that we could do that too. Gervais concludes his piece by comparing Reaney to John Keating, the English teacher in the film *Dead Poets Society,* saying that like Keating, Reaney 'turns our thoughts upside down, disrupts our vision, makes us examine and challenge everything around us, and to take nothing for granted' (2). Again in Blake's terms, Reaney does everything he can to help us to perceive actively.

This approach is a far cry from the methods ordered by the art manual that Reaney holds in the photograph on the *Windsor Review* cover. True to his 'permanent structure of ideas', in Frye's phrase, Reaney's teaching brings into proximity, as magnetic poles, students and materials related to the subject of study. Gervais had this experience in a personal register, during a visit to Reaney's farm. Reaney, he writes,

> took me on a walk around the property and almost at every step, one could trace particular things about the farm, its pond and wildflowers and the barn, back to his stories and poetry. In a curious way, his autobiography unfolded right here, at each and every step, whether it be the field that he crossed on his way to school, or the pond, or the wildflowers or the barn, or that place in the house where he sat reading *Wuthering Heights* as a child.
>
> It was there his literature took shape, took flight.

Gervais then goes on to relate what he learned from this peripatetic lesson about Reaney:

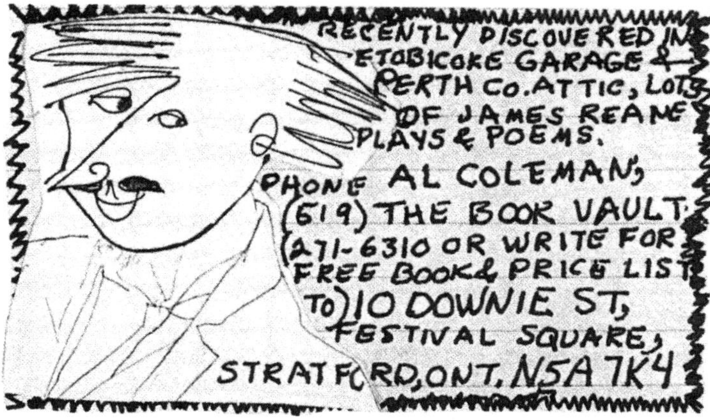

'Some ad I made for my remainders that's myself at all ages at once. Pretty sharp beak, right?' (1985)

> In a way, it was like looking into his soul.
>
> And that's the point of it. Reaney knows we're alive with stories, with histories. They swarm about us, and we can't go on till we begin to tell them. If you just take a look around your own house, you'll see what I mean. Reaney's done it, not in any solipsistic manner, but in a way to illuminate the ordinary, the everyday life with all its extraordinary moments. (2)

In a sense, then, Reaney teaches us to perceive the extraordinary in the ordinary by doing so himself, by writing and playing, drawing and acting, and teaching.

The *Windsor Review* issue featuring Reaney presents a good many more items of interest, including Reaney's self-portrait on an advertisement he made to try to sell copies of his books that he had accumulated. The text below the ad was written by Reaney. The figure on the left is a drawing he did; it appears several times earlier with the title 'Rural Dandy'.

From 1980 to 1983 I worked on a doctoral thesis with Reaney's guidance. The thesis grew out of his graduate course, Ontario Literature and Culture. This course functioned similarly to the way Gervais's visit to Reaney's farm did. The class met weekly at a large table in Reaney's office, in the tower of University College at Western. The office was a crammed collection of books, journals, encyclopaedias, maps, artwork, and artefacts of all sorts. It was fascinating to browse. Much of the material related to topics that made up our course, it turned out, and I recall borrowing some items as research sources for several projects. One such project evolved into my thesis on David Willson's writing. As with Gervais's farm tour, Reaney opened up to his students worlds of possibilities. He knew very well the contents of his library, but his knowledge was not the focus of attention. Instead, as a teacher he shared his enthusiasm about the manifold stories implicit in his collection, in an effort, as he used to say, echoing Blake, to rouse our faculties, to inspire us to 'work the documentary pumps' with these documents, in order to do our own cultural work.

Along with this encouragement and freedom to explore, Reaney also supplied his students with expectations of rigour and thoroughness in what we did. My reading for the Willson thesis, for example, included all of the philosophical and religious background material by Jakob Boehme, Emmanuel Swedenborg, and George Fox; Quaker theology and history, particularly in the US and Canada; Upper Canadian history and politics; genealogical materials on the members of the Children of Peace, the group that Willson led from 1812 until his death in 1866; and all of Willson's hymns, sermons, poems and speeches — and this is a man who claimed that 'the children's bread is ever new', so he wrote new hymns for virtually every service held in their Temple at Sharon, Ontario. Part of my thesis research turned into helping catalogue the masses of Willson documents that were stored in Sharon; another instructive bypath was my being asked to edit the Toronto Historical Society's journal, *The York Pioneer*. Then there was getting the thesis written and approved by Reaney and my other readers. I present all of this detail in order to illustrate that Reaney's teaching methods were effective, and much like those of Old Strictus, the goslings' teacher described in the July eclogue of *A Suit of Nettles*. Valancy recalls that Old Strictus 'taught us to know the most wonderful list of things'. Once the student geese had learned the list 'forwards and backwards', and 'they knew all that a young goose was supposed to know, … it was as joyous a moment as if they had been reborn into another world' (44–45).

'Two Chapters from an Emblem Book' is a fragment of the larger, never-finished emblem book. Who knows how many chapters Reaney might have projected? The two chapters are all he published. Possibly, he never did plan to add any more emblems. Deliberately leaving a work unfinished has been an artistic strategy since at least the Florentine Renaissance, for instance in the '*non finito*' sculptures of Donatello (1386–1466) and Michelangelo (1475–1564). The Romantics adopted the technique, famously in poems such as 'Christabel' and 'Kubla Khan' by Samuel Taylor Coleridge (1772–1834), and 'Don Juan' by Lord George Gordon Byron (1788–1824). Modernists expanded the sense of being 'unfinished' from meaning 'cut off before an ending recognizable as such', to include 'fragmented'. The poetry of T.S. Eliot (1888–1965) and Ezra Pound (1885–1972), the artworks of Pablo Picasso (1881–1973) and Georges Braque (1882–1963), and the musical compositions of Igor Stravinsky (1882–1971) and John Cage (1912–1992), are examples of the use of bricolage, the assembling of miscellaneous bits and pieces without explicit narrative connections, or any other 'beginning/middle/ending' structure. Modernists left the assembly process to the people who seek meaning in their art. In Renaissance terms, this putting together of meaning would be called 'wit'. Reaney's emblem making, as we have noted, takes shape on the bases of both Renaissance and Modernist traditions. The incomplete quality of 'Two Chapters from an Emblem Book' lets us know that there is more here than meets the eye.

Where, then, do Reaney's emblems leave us? I have tried to show that the ten emblems comprise a full cycle of meaning. The tenth emblem, 'The Hat', signals this unity with its circular illustration. Suggesting that the unity is cyclical, the circle shape appears, albeit smaller and in combination with other shapes, in 'The Castle', the emblem 'following' the tenth, with which the series starts. But there is a break after the tenth emblem/ before the first, not only visually in the altered circle, but thematically, between the threshold of apocalypse in 'The Hat' and the 'Castle' emblem's 'ground plan/For a castle called Man'. The ten emblems thus do not form a 'closed circle', to use Northrop Frye's term in his description of the Bible's ending. His explanation can also be applied to the overall shape of Reaney's emblems:

> The final comprehension of the Bible's meaning is in the spark of illumination between its closing anode and its opening cathode, and if that gap were not there the Bible would not stimulate the

> imagination to the effort of comprehension which recreates instead of passively following the outline of a vision. (*Fearful Symmetry* 386)

Both great teachers, Frye and Reaney were Modernists too, and might be expected to share this understanding of an ending as unfinished, as an invitation to engage in working out the consequences of such a disjuncture evident in a patently circular form.

Reaney composed a tribute to Frye the day after his teacher's death on January 23, 1991, titled 'Northrop Frye: He educated our imagination'. One of his 'folkloric' reminiscences about Frye employs an image similar to that of the anode/cathode and to Reaney's own magnet system. He recalls that Frye was famous for the use of silence in his lectures.

> These silences were signs that the pupils were being called upon to fill in a gap and they usually did impelled as much by the absence of the Word as its presence.

The silent gaps between Reaney's emblems, and also within them, between the illustrations and the words, are clear appeals to us to see what we can make of them. As we have discovered, there is an abundance to be made.

---

1. Invisible in the photograph, behind Reaney's pianist's pointer finger is information about the book's printer, 'The T. Eaton Co. Ltd. Toronto. Canada'.

References

Adams, Hazard. *William Blake on His Poetry and Painting: A Study of* A Descriptive Catalogue, *Other Prose Writings and* Jerusalem. Jefferson, NC: McFarland, 2011.

Alciato, Andrea. *Emblematum Liber.* Augsburg: Heinrich Steyner, 1531.

Aristotle. *Poetics.* Trans. Leon Golden. *The Critical Tradition: Classic Texts and Contemporary Trends,* 2nd ed. Ed. David H. Richter. Boston: Bedford, 1998. 42–64.

Arnheim, Rudolf. *Visual Thinking.* 1969. Berkeley: University of California Press, 1997.

Atwood, Margaret. 'Reaney Collected'. Review of *Poems,* ed. Germaine Warkentin. *Canadian Literature* 57 (1973): 113–17.

Ayre, John. 'Frye's geometry of thought: Building the great wheel'. *University of Toronto Quarterly* 70.4 (2001): 825–38.

Bath, Michael. *Speaking Pictures: English Emblem Books and Renaissance Culture.* London: Longman, 1994.

Beckwith, John. 'Musical Quotations in *Taptoo!*' *Sonneck Society Bulletin* 21. Fall 1995: 5–7.

Berger, John. *Ways of Seeing.* London: BBC/Penguin, 1972.

Blake, William. 'Auguries of Innocence'. Keynes, *Blake: Complete Writings.* 431–34.

——. *Blake's Poetry and Designs: Illuminated Works, Other Writings, Criticism.* 1979. Ed. M.L. Johnson and John E. Grant. New York: Norton, 2008.

——. *Blake: Complete Writings with Variant Readings.* Ed. Geoffrey Keynes. London: Oxford, 1969.

——. *The Letters of William Blake.* Ed. Geoffrey Keynes. New York: Macmillan, 1956.

——. *The Marriage of Heaven and Hell.* Intro. Geoffrey Keynes. London: Oxford University Press, 1975.

——. *The Notebook of William Blake: A Photographic and Typographic Facsimile.* Ed. David V. Erdman. Oxford: Clarendon, 1973.

——. 'To Dr Trusler 23 August 1799'. Keynes, *Blake: Complete Writings.* 793.

Bloom, Harold. Commentary. *The Poetry and Prose of William Blake.* Ed. David V. Erdman. Garden City, NY: Doubleday, 1965.

Bunyan, John. *The Pilgrim's Progress from this World to that which is to come.* 1678. Ed. J.B. Wharey and Roger Sharrock. Oxford: Clarendon, 1960.

Burke, Edmund. *A Philosophical Inquiry into the Origins of Our Ideas of the Sublime and the Beautiful.* Ed. J.T. Boulton. London: Routledge, 1958.

Campbell, Wanda. 'Alchemy in Ontario: Reaney's *Twelve Letters to a Small Town*'. *Canadian Literature* 151 (1996): 102–17.

——. '"To Flow Like You": An Interview with James Reaney'. *Windsor Review* 29.1 (1996): 9–21.

Cirlot, J.E. *A Dictionary of Symbols.* Trans. Jack Sage. New York: Philosophical Library, 1962.

Cotrupi, Caterina Nella. *Northrop Frye and the Poetics of Process.* Toronto: University of Toronto Press, 2000.

cummings, e.e. 'The Wind Is A Lady With'. *&*. 1925.

'Crystal'. OED Online. December 2012. Oxford University Press.

Daly, Peter M. *Literature in the Light of the Emblem: Structural Parallels between the Emblem and Literature in the Sixteenth and Seventeenth Centuries.* 1979. 2nd edition. Toronto: University of Toronto Press, 1998.

——, ed. *The English Emblem and the Continental Tradition.* New York: AMS, 1988.

Denham, Robert D. *Northrop Frye & Critical Method.* Pennsylvania State University, 1978.

De Selincourt, Ernest. Introduction. *Spenser: Poetical Works.* Ed. J.C. Smith and E. de Selincourt. 1912. London: Oxford University Press, 1969. vii–lxvii.

Dudek, Louis. 'A Problem of Meaning'. *Canadian Literature* 59 (Winter 1974): 16–29.

Edgerton, Samuel Y. *The Mirror, the Window, and the Telescope: How Renaissance Linear Perspective Changed Our Vision of the Universe.* Ithaca: Cornell University Press, 2009.

Elkins, James. *The Poetics of Perspective.* Ithaca: Cornell University Press, 1994.

'Emblem'. OED Online. December 2012. Oxford University Press.

Fisher, Peter Francis. *The Valley of Vision: Blake as Prophet and Revolutionary.* Ed. Northrop Frye. Toronto: University of Toronto Press, 1961.

Foster Damon, Samuel. *A Blake Dictionary: The Ideas and Symbols of William Blake.* 1965. Rev. Ed. Morris Eaves. Hanover, NH: University Press of New England, 1988.

Frazer, James George, Sir. *The Golden Bough.* New York: Macmillan, 1922.

Freeman, Rosemary. *English Emblem Books.* New York: Octagon, 1966.

Frye, Northrop. *Anatomy of Criticism: Four Essays.* 1957. Princeton: Princeton University Press. 1971.

——. 'Blake's Treatment of the Archetype'. *English Institute Essays: 1950.* New York: Columbia University Press, 1951. 170–96. Rpt. in Blake, *Blake's Poetry and Designs.* 524–36.

——. 'The Archetypes of Literature'. *Fables of Identity: Studies in Poetic Mythology.* New York: Harcourt, 1963. 7–20.

——. *Fearful Symmetry: A Study of William Blake.* 1947. Princeton: Princeton University Press, 1970.

——. *The Modern Century.* Toronto Oxford University Press, 1967.

Gardner, Helen. *The Metaphysical Poets.* Oxford: Penguin, 1957.

Gerry, Thomas M.F. '"Imagining Out Things": The Act of Vision in James Reaney's *Alphabet*'. *University of Toronto Quarterly* 70.4 (Fall 2001): 857–68.

Gilchrist, Alexander. *Life of William Blake, 'Pictor Ignotus'.* 2 vols. London: Macmillan, 1863.

Glickman, Susan. *The Picturesque and the Sublime: A Poetics of the Canadian Landscape.* Montreal: McGill-Queen's University Press, 1998.

Gombrich, E.H. *Art and Illusion: A Study in the Psychology of Pictorial Representation.* Princeton: Princeton University Press, 1960.

Graham, David. 'Emblema multiplex: Towards a Typology of Emblematic Forms, Structures and Functions'. *Emblem Scholarship Directions and Development: A Tribute to Gabriel Hornstein.* Imago Figurata Studies Vol. 5. Ed. Peter M. Daly. Turnhout, Belgium: Brepols, 2005. 131–58.

Grant, George. 'Thinking about Technology'. *Technology and Justice.* Toronto: Anansi, 1986. 11–34.

Green, Henry. *Shakespeare and the Emblem Writers: An Exposition of Their Similarities of Thought and Expression.* London: Trübner, 1870.

Griggs, Terry. 'James Reaney's Giants'. *Approaches to the Work of James Reaney.* Ed. Stan Dragland. Toronto: ECW Press, 1938. 15–31.

Hagstrum, Jean H. *The Sister Arts: The Tradition of Literary Pictorialism and English Poetry from Dryden to Gray.* 1958. Chicago: University of Chicago Press, 1987.

——. *William Blake, Poet and Painter: An Introduction to the Illuminated Verse.* Chicago: University of Chicago Press, 1964.

'Hermaphroditic'. OED Online. December 2102. Oxford University Press.

Hobbema, Meindert. *The Alley at Middelharnis.* 1689. National Gallery, London. Number 830.

Hobbes, Thomas. *Leviathan or The Matter, Forme, & Power of a Common-Wealth Ecclesiastical and Civill.* London: Andrew Crooke, 1651.

'Ignis fatuus'. OED Online. December 2012. Oxford University Press.

Izquierdo, Sebastián. *Praxis exercitiorum spiritualium P.N.S. Ignatii.* Rome: Varesius, 1678.

Jonas, Raymond. *France and the Cult of the Sacred Heart: An Epic Tale for Modern Times.* Studies on the History of Society and Culture 39. Berkeley: University of California Press, 2000.

Jung, C.G. *Psychology and Alchemy.* 1944. Trans. R.F.C. Hull. *The Collected Works of C.G. Jung,* vol. 12. London: Routledge, 1953.

——. *The Red Book (Liber novus).* Ed. Sonu Shamdasani. Trans. Mark Kyburz, John Peck, and Sonu Shamdasani. New York: Norton, 2009.

Kellogg, Rhoda. *Analyzing Children's Art.* Palo Alto: National Press, 1969.

——, with Scott O'Dell. *The Psychology of Children's Art.* New York: Random, 1967.

Krieger, Murray. *Ekphrasis: The Illusion of the Natural Sign.* Baltimore: Johns Hopkins University Press, 1992.

Larrissy, Edward. *Blake and Modern Literature.* Houndmills, Basingstoke, Hampshire, UK: Palgrave Macmillan, 2006.

Lee, Alvin A. *James Reaney.* New York Twayne, 1968.

Libbrecht, Kenneth G. *A Guide to Snowflakes.* 'Fernlike Stellar Dendrites'. http://www.its.caltech.edu/˜atomic/snowcrystals/class/class.htm.

Lindley, David, ed. *The Court Masque.* Manchester: Manchester University Press, 1984.

Macpherson, Jay. Rev. of *Listen to the Wind. The Canadian Forum* (September) 1966: 136–7. Rpt. as Introduction. *Listen to the Wind,* by James Reaney. 3–7.

Malraux, André. *The Voices of Silence.* 1953. Trans. Stuart Gilbert. Princeton: Princeton University Press, 1990.

Manning, John. *The Emblem.* London: Reaktion, 2002.

McKay, Jean. 'What on earth are you doing, Sir?' *ArtScape* 5 (June 2006): 10.

Métraux, Alfred. *Voodoo in Haiti.* Trans. Hugo Charteris. London: André Deutsch, 1959.

Miller, Clarence H. 'Donne's "A Nocturnall upon S. Lucies Day" and the Nocturns of Matins'. *Studies in English Literature, 1500–1900* 6.1 (Winter, 1966): 77–86.

Miller, J. Hillis. *Illustration.* Cambridge: Harvard University Press, 1992.

Milton, John. *Paradise Lost* (1667). Ed. Philip Pullman. Oxford University Press, 2005.

Mitchell, W. J. T. *Iconology.* Chicago: University of Chicago Press, 1986.

——. 'Imperial Landscape'. *Landscape and Power.* Ed. W. J. T. Mitchell. Chicago: University of Chicago Press, 1994. 5–34.

——. *Picture Theory: Essays on Verbal and Visual Representation.* Chicago: University of Chicago Press, 1994.

Morgan, David. 'The Protestant Struggle with the Image'. *Religion Online.* http://www.religion-online.org/cgi-bin/relsearchd.dll/showarticle?item_id=840.

Nellist, Brian. '*The Pilgrim's Progress* and Allegory'. The Pilgrim's Progress: *Critical and Historical Views.* Ed. Vincent Newey. Liverpool: Liverpool University Press, 1980.

Palmer, Samuel. *Samuel Palmer's Valley of Vision.* Intro. Geoffrey Grigson. London: Phoenix House, 1960.

Panofsky, Erwin. *Studies in Iconology: Humanistic Themes in the Art of the Renaissance.* 1939. New York: Harper, 1962.

Parker, Gerald D. *How to Play: The Theatre of James Reaney.* Toronto: ECW Press, 1991.

Plato. *Phaedrus.* Trans. H.N. Fowler. *The Rhetorical Tradition: Readings from Classical Times to the Present.* Ed. Patricia Bizzell and Bruce Herzberg. New York: St. Martin's, 1990. 113–43.

——. *The Republic,* Book X. Trans. Benjamin Jowett. Bizzell and Herzberg. 21–29.

Praz, Mario. *Studies in Seventeenth Century Imagery.* 1939. 2nd edition. Rome: Edizioni di Storia e Letteratura, 1964.

Quarles, Francis. *Hieroglyphikes.* 1638. Ed. John Horden. London: Scolar, 1969.

——. *Emblems Divine and Moral: Together with Hieroglyphicks of the Life of Man.* 1634. London: Trapp, 1777.

Reaney, James, ed. *Alphabet: A Semiannual Devoted to the Iconography of the Imagination.* 1–20. London, 1960–71.

——. 'An Evening with Babble and Doodle: Presentations of Poetry'. *Canadian Literature* 12 (Spring 1962): 37–43.

——. *The Box Social and Other Stories.* Erin: Porcupine's Quill, 1996.

——. 'A Cellar Song'. *Poetry* 94 (1959): 380.

——. 'Northrop Frye: He educated our imagination.' *Toronto Star* 24 January 1991: A27.

——. 'The Identifier Effect'. *The CEA (College English Association) Critic* 42.2 (1980): 26–31.

——. 'The Influence of Spenser on Yeats'. Diss. University of Toronto, 1958.

——. 'James Crerar Reaney'. *Gale Contemporary Authors Autobiography Series.* Vol. 15. Detroit: Gale, 1991. 295–309.

——. *Listen to the Wind.* Vancouver: Talonbooks, 1972.

——. *One-man Masque. Two Plays by James Reaney.* London: Ergo Productions, 2003. 37–59.

——. *Performance Poems.* Goderich: Moonstone, 1990.

——. *Poems.* Ed. Germaine Warkentin. Toronto: New Press, 1972.

——. *The Red Heart.* Toronto: McClelland, 1949.

——. *Scripts: Librettos for Operas and Other Musical Works.* Toronto: Coach House, 2004.

——. 'Search for an Undiscovered Alphabet'. *Canadian Art* 22.4 (1965): 38–41.

——. *Souwesto Home.* London: Brick Books, 2005.

——. *A Suit of Nettles.* 1958. Erin: Porcupine's Quill, 2010.

——. *Taptoo!* 1999. *Scripts.* 301–56.

——. 'Ten Years at Play'. *Canadian Literature* 41 (Summer 1969): 53–61.

——. 'Vision in Canada?' *University of Toronto Quarterly* 70.4 (2001): 937–46.

Reaney, James Stewart. *James Reaney.* Toronto: Gage, 1977.

Rigaud, Milo. *Vè-vè: Diagrammes Rituels de Voudou.* New York: French and European Publications, 1974.

Schell, Winston G. Interview with James Reaney (c. 1974–75). *Parts of People in These Parts.* London: n.p., 1985.

Sharman-Burke, Juliet. *The Complete Book of Tarot.* London: Pan, 1985.

Sharrock, Roger. 'Bunyan and the English Emblem Writers'. *Review of English Studies* 21.82 (1945): 105–16.

Sheffield, Betty. 'Is snow a mineral?' National Snow and Ice Data Center User Services. November 2002. http://nsidc.org/snow/faq.html.

Stingle, Richard. "all the old levels': Reaney and Frye'. *Approaches to the Work of James Reaney.* Ed. Stan Dragland. Toronto: ECW Press, 1983. 32–62.

——. (Unpublished) Notes for an English 022 Lecture on Emblems. University of Western Ontario. 13 Sept. 1979.

'Tattoo'. OED Online. June 2011. Oxford University Press.

Tipton, Ian. 'Berkeley, George'. *Routledge Encyclopedia of Philosophy* online. London: Routledge 1998. http://www.rep.routledge.com/article/DA006.

Vaughan, William. *Samuel Palmer, 1805–1881*: Vision and Landscape. London: British Museum Press. 2005.

'Vorpal'. OED Online. June 2011. Oxford University Press.

Voss, Angela. 'The Music of the Spheres — Ficino and Renaissance Harmonia'. http://www.rvrcd.co.uk/catalogue/ficino/fessay1.htm.

Walker, Craig Stewart. *The Buried Astrolabe: Canadian Dramatic Imagination and Western Tradition.* Montreal: McGill-Queen's University Press, 2001.

Walls, Peter. *Music in the English Courtly Masque, 1604–1640.* Oxford: Oxford University Press, 1996.

Warkentin, Germaine. Introduction. *Poems* by James Reaney. vii-xviii.

——. '"Out of Spenser and the Common Tongue" James Reaney's "A Suit of Nettles" (1958)'. *James Reaney.* http://www.jamesreaney.com/gallery/warkentin/.

Whitney, Geffrey. *A Choice of Emblemes, and other devises, For the moste part gathered out of sundrie writers, Englished and Moralized.* Leyden: Christopher Plantyn, 1586.

'Will-o'-the-wisp'. OED Online. December 2012. Oxford University Press.

Wilson, Mark A. 'Manganese oxide dendrites on a limestone bedding plane from Solnhofen, Germany'. http://en.wikipedia.org/wiki/File:Dendrites01.jpg.

Woodman, Ross. *James Reaney.* Toronto: McClelland, 1971.

Acknowledgements

Heartfelt thanks to the following people. I was going to try to categorize them as either having done indispensable practical work on this project, or as having shared their enthusiasm and inspiration. However, practical/personal turns out to be a spectrum, so here they are in a list: Susan Wallace, James Stewart Reaney, James Crerar Reaney, Colleen Thibaudeau, Peter Rich, Elke Inkster, Tim Inkster, Tom Smart, Kathleen Gerry, Natalie Gerry, Scot Bishop, Stephanie Small, Doris Cowan, Germaine Warkentin, Amanda Jamieson. The Laurentian University Research Fund provided financial assistance to obtain the illustrations other than those by James Reaney.

Page 2: James Reaney printing *Alphabet*, January 1967. *London Free Press*/Sun Media Corporation.

Page 14: From *Choice of Emblemes*, by Geffrey Whitney. Reproduced with the permission of Rare Books and Manuscripts, Special Collections Library, Pennsylvania State University Libraries.

Page 38: 'Prisoners in the Underworld'. The Thomas Fisher Rare Book Library, University of Toronto.

Page 63: 'The Swan and Harp'. © The Worshipful Company of Musicians, 2 London Wall Buildings, London, UK.

Page 73: *The Avenue at Middelharnis*. © The National Gallery, London, UK.

Page 76: *Newton*, by William Blake. © Tate, London 2012.

Page 92: Fernlike stellar dendrite. © Kenneth G. Libbrecht, SnowCrystals.com.

Page 99: 'Squaring of the circle to make the sexes one whole', Michael Maier, rpt. in Jung's *Psychology and Alchemy*. With the permission of the Getty Research Institute, Los Angeles.

Page 142: The vèvè of the snake god, Damballah-wèdo and his consort Aïda-wèdo. From *Voodoo in Haiti* by Alfred Métraux, originally published by Andre Deutsch. With the permission of the Carlton Publishing group.

Page 144: The symbols of various *loa*. From *Voodoo in Haiti* by Alfred Métraux, originally published by Andre Deutsch. With the permission of the Carlton Publishing group.

Page 146: The vèvè of the goddess Erzulie Freda. From *Voodoo in Haiti* by Alfred Métraux, originally published by Andre Deutsch. With the permission of the Carlton Publishing group.

Page 155: Gadsden Flag. © Dannyconlan | Dreamstime.com.

Page 176: An Emblematic Photograph of James Reaney. *Windsor Review: A Journal of the Arts* 29.1 (1996): cover. Photograph by Marty Gervais.

The following is a list of James Reaney's works. For so generously permitting the use of these emblems and other images, thanks to James Stewart Reaney and Susan Wallace.

Cover: After an original watercolour titled *The Typewriter.*

Page 30: 'stdfraort semper'. *Twelve Letters to a Small Town,* 1962. Rpt. in *Poems,* 1972. 210.

Page 34: The Castle. Cover of *Poetry* (Chicago) 115.3 (December 1969).

Page 58: The Farm. *Poetry* (Chicago) 115.3 (December 1969): 151.

Page 70: Egypt. *Poetry* (Chicago) 115.3 (December 1969): 150.

Page 88: Within Within. *Poetry* (Chicago) 115.3 (December 1969): 152.

Page 98: The Tree. *Poetry* (Chicago) 115.3 (December 1969): 153.

Page 110: The Riddle. *Armadillo* 2 (1970).

Page 119: *The Artist & Table* — 'Brush'.

Page 120: *The Painter's Table* — 'Pen'.

Page 121: *The Poet's Table* — 'Frond'.

Page 128: Windlady. *Armadillo* 2 (1970).

Page 140: Baron Samedi Porte Baton. *Armadillo* 2 (1970).

Page 158: The Last House. *Armadillo* 2 (1970).

Page 166: The Hat. *Armadillo* 2 (1970).

Page 181: Ad for Remainders, 1985. *Windsor Review: A Journal of the Arts* 29.1 (1996): 15.

Page 185: Butterfly party favour created by James Reaney on the occasion of his twenty-first birthday.

Thomas Gerry first encountered the work of the poet, playwright and painter James Reaney while studying at the University of Toronto, but it was his experience of performing in community theatre productions of Reaney's plays that deepened his interest in Reaney's writing. When Gerry received his Ph.D. from the University of Western Ontario in 1983 under Reaney's supervision, he began a lasting friendship with Reaney and his family.

Since 1981 Gerry has taught at Laurentian University, where he edited *Arachnē,* a bilingual interdisciplinary journal of language and literature, from 1996 to 2000. He sits on the advisory board for *Studies in Canadian Literature,* regularly reviews books for scholarly journals, and has published numerous poems, articles, and several music recordings. His fascination with interdisciplinary arts led him to the works of Anna Jameson, Elizabeth Simcoe, Joni Mitchell, David Milne and others who combine writing or music with visual art. His article about Reaney's visual and musical imagination formed the basis for *The Emblems of James Reaney.*